Programme Making for Radio

Programme Making for Radio offers trainee radio broadcasters and their instructors focused practical guidelines to the professional techniques applied to the making of radio shows, explaining how specific radio programmes are made and the conventions and techniques required to produce them. The book describes how and why these methods are applied through the use of a behind-the-scenes glimpse at working practices and procedures used in the industry. It considers the constraints and incentives that limit or stimulate creativity and innovation within programme production.

Programme Making for Radio examines the individual roles and responsibilities of the whole production team and the importance of team-working skills. Chapters focus on the specific requirements of specialist programmes and offer advice from a range of programme makers working in local and national broadcasting. There is a case study example that follows the progress of a Feature Programme from pitching the original idea, through assembling material to final transmission.

Programme Making for Radio includes:

- a clear description of the role of each member of the programme-making team, their duties and responsibilities

- practical tips on interviewing, mixing and presenting

- explanations of the key elements that make up a radio programme such as clips, wraps, packages, features and interviews with a full glossary of technical terms.

The book is informed, accessible and comprehensive, covering the whole range of skills needed by the radio professional in the studio and on location.

Jim Beaman is Senior Lecturer in Radio at University of Sunderland and has worked as an instructor with BBC Radio Training. His broadcasting career includes presenting, producing and reporting for BBC Radio. He is the author of *Interviewing for Radio* published by Routledge.

Media Skills

SERIES EDITOR: RICHARD KEEBLE, LINCOLN UNIVERSITY
SERIES ADVISERS: WYNFORD HICKS AND JENNY McKAY

The *Media Skills* series provides a concise and thorough introduction to a rapidly changing media landscape. Each book is written by media and journalism lecturers or experienced professionals and is a key resource for a particular industry. Offering helpful advice and information and using practical examples from print, broadcast and digital media, as well as discussing ethical and regulatory issues, *Media Skills* books are essential guides for students and media professionals.

English for Journalists, 2nd edition
Wynford Hicks

Writing for Journalists
Wynford Hicks with Sally Adams and Harriett Gilbert

Interviewing for Radio
Jim Beaman

Web Production for Writers and Journalists, 2nd edition
Jason Whittaker

Ethics for Journalists
Richard Keeble

Scriptwriting for the Screen
Charlie Moritz

Interviewing for Journalists
Sally Adams, with an introduction and additional material by Wynford Hicks

Researching for Television and Radio
Adèle Emm

Reporting for Journalists
Chris Frost

Subediting for Journalists
Wynford Hicks and Tim Holmes

Designing for Newspapers and Magazines
Chris Frost

Writing for Broadcast Journalists
Rick Thompson

Freelancing For Television and Radio
Leslie Mitchell

Find more details of current *Media Skills* books and forthcoming titles at
www.producing.routledge.com

Programme Making for Radio

Jim Beaman

Routledge
Taylor & Francis Group

LONDON AND NEW YORK

First published 2006
by Routledge
2 Park Square, Milton Park, Abingdon, Oxon OX14 4RN

Simultaneously published in the USA and Canada
by Routledge
270 Madison Ave, New York, NY 10016

Routledge is an imprint of the Taylor & Francis Group, an informa business

© 2006 Jim Beaman

Typeset in Garamond 3 by Keystroke, 28 High Street, Tettenhall, Wolverhampton
Printed and bound in Great Britain by TJ International Ltd, Padstow, Cornwall

British Library Cataloguing in Publication Data
A catalogue record for this book is available from the British Library

Library of Congress Cataloging in Publication Data
Beaman, Jim, 1949–
    Programme making for radio / Jim Beaman.
        p. cm. — (Media skills)
    Includes bibliographical references and index.
    1. Radio—Production and direction. I. Title. II. Series.
    PN1991.75.B43 2006
    791.4402′32—dc22   2006009670

ISBN 10: 0–415–36571–6 (hbk)
ISBN 10: 0–415–36572–4 (pbk)

ISBN 13: 978–0–415–36571–0 (hbk)
ISBN 13: 978–0–415–36572–7 (pbk)

For Sarah and in memory of Peggy

Contents

Acknowledgements

My gratitude and respect to the following friends and colleagues in broadcasting, training and education who contributed so generously of their time, knowledge and expertise. Thank you for your patience and understanding:

Helen Galley, Fran Acheson, Sarah Fuller, Gurindar Barar, Tony Fisher, Sally Abrahams, Andy Cartwright, Bob Turner, Martin Conboy, Paul Jenner, Matt Foster, Richard Berry, Caroline Mitchell, Graham Cook, Caroline Kingsmill, Jo Tyler, Katy McDonald, Alec Blackman, Guy Starkey, Neil Calvert, Grant Lowery, Sarah Urban, Matt Horne, Tony Bonner, Warwick Pilmer and Catherine Bott.

My thanks to the Centre for Research in Media and Cultural Studies at the School of Arts, Design, Media and Culture of the University of Sunderland and to the staff and students of the Radio Department at the University of Sunderland.

Introduction

Examining your own listening history is perhaps a good place to start if you are contemplating becoming a radio programme producer or planning to study radio as an academic or practical subject. Try to remember your earliest memories of hearing the radio. As youngsters most of us will have been aware of voices and music coming out of a radio somewhere in the house: the choice of station received and the programme we heard broadcast would have been selected not by us but by an older member of the household. My parents for example were keen on the Light Programme provided at that time by the BBC. So my UK 1950s childhood sound-track was made up of music programmes like *Housewives Choice* and *Music While You Work* during the week, *Children's Favourites* on Saturdays and on Sundays we listened to *Family Favourites*, *The Billy Cotton Band Show* and comedy shows like *Round the Horne* and *The Navy Lark*.

Despite being a member of the television generation radio still held a fascination for me, and together with the help of a friend and his father's tape recorder we tried to perform and record our own versions of our favourite programmes.

Later when I was given a portable transistor radio as a birthday present I was able to make my own listening choices. I became a regular listener to Radio Luxembourg in the evenings and the pirate stations transmitting from ships anchored outside British territorial waters who broadcast the kind of music I liked and programmes presented by the kind of DJs who spoke my language and were in touch with youth culture. In the 1960s it was announced that the BBC would be launching its own pop music station, Radio 1. I wrote a letter to them suggesting they would need some new DJs and asked if I could be one of them. To my surprise they replied requesting a demo tape of me presenting a programme. I went out and bought the latest top five singles and wrote a script of my show. I borrowed an open-reel tape recorder and microphone, emptied my wardrobe – which was to act as a makeshift studio – and recorded my little show. Needless to say I received a very polite letter of rejection, but this didn't stop me listening to the station and my particular favourites John Peel and Kenny Everett.

If I were to attempt the same exercise today I would be able to make use of the free downloads of digital editing and mixing software which would help me to produce a professional-sounding programme.

Once I had left home I gradually started to listen more regularly to BBC Radio 4, becoming appreciative of speech radio and developing an addiction for *Today*, *Kaleidoscope*, *Book at Bedtime* and any radio drama.

As a student in Higher Education I was given the opportunity to learn the practical skills required to make radio programmes and to experiment with audio to my heart's content (be aware that the opportunities to experiment do become more limited once you start working for a mainstream broadcaster). So once I knew what went on in front of and behind the microphone I began listening with a new intensity.

The biggest change to my listening habits came when I started working for BBC local radio and became immersed in the output and the audience of my own station to the exclusion of pretty well everything on the airwaves.

Fran Acheson, who is Learning Executive, Journalism and Radio at BBC Training and Development, offers the following advice on their web site to aspiring programme makers:

> *Listen, listen, listen. Listen to as much different radio as you can. If you want to get into music radio, listen to Radio 1, 1Extra, 6Music and commercial radio. If you can, get your hands on recordings and listen to the fabulous DJs of old. When I started I asked everyone I was working with: 'What are the best radio programmes you've ever heard?' I came up with a list and went to BBC archives and I ordered all of them and spent a fortnight listening. I think I learnt an awful lot about radio.*

Once you know how radio programmes are made you tend to listen with a more educated ear to what is coming out of the speakers because you understand what is going on behind the scenes of the production. Later, as I developed awareness and an understanding of the power and potential of radio, I once again became promiscuous in my listening habits and as the number of stations continued to grow I seemed to be forever retuning the dial.

Most radio listening is a secondary activity. You listen when you are brushing your teeth, eating or driving. Sometimes you should simply sit down and listen in a more focused way to fully appreciate the content within and the craftsmanship applied to a programme. You know when you have just listened to a good radio programme. The magic of the medium has engaged your imagination and left you with a feeling of satisfaction. You have been personally entertained, stimulated, informed and perhaps fascinated by an original and evocative collection of voices, sounds and music coming out of the dark. Why did you enjoy it? Why did it sound so good? It can be hard to translate what you hear into the useable skills that enable you to make a radio programme that others will want to listen to.

This book will hopefully help you to dissect and evaluate a range of factual radio programmes (I have not included drama, sitcoms, panel games and light entertainment in general) by revealing the techniques used by programme makers that you could adapt for your own use. If you are passionate about radio you will of course be an avid and enquiring listener who not only absorbs and appreciates the content of a programme but also asks how it was made. This book should be a starting point for your investigations. If you hope to become a radio professional learn as much as possible from a range of sources, in particular get to know radio programme makers – they are the best people to talk to you if you want to know how programmes are produced. You may even be lucky enough to find a mentor who will guide you through the pleasures and pitfalls of programme production because they remember what it was like to be new to the industry. The more you listen to and discuss programmes the more you will get to know about the medium, its language and working practices. Read the trade papers, magazines and media supplements in newspapers to find out the latest developments, debates and issues affecting the medium. What do the critics have to say about certain programmes in their previews and reviews? If you get the chance go along and join the audience at a recording of a radio programme. Some comedy shows, panel games and discussion programmes travel around the country recording editions of their programmes in front of audiences. You can learn a lot about how it is done by watching them at work and then listening to the broadcast and comparing what was recorded and eventually edited out before transmission. You can access station web sites where you will find information about their staff roles and experience history and about their programmes and what you can expect to hear. Sometimes you can take a virtual tour of the studios which will give you an idea of the equipment that is used by the programme makers. Try to get some work experience or shadowing opportunities. Many broadcasters, engineers and producers have started their careers on hospital, college or Restricted Service Licence (RSL) stations. Practical experience and appropriate skills of applicants play a major role in the appointments process, plus the more hands-on experience and practice you are able to get the greater the understanding of techniques and the development of your potential for creativity within your future productions.

Students are inevitably required to analyse and comment on what they hear whether it be programmes made by professionals, other trainee broadcasters or indeed their own productions. Listening to your own work in the presence of your peers during playback sessions can be daunting, and giving feedback to others about their work can be a difficult process. So perhaps a few guidelines on listening to and discussing radio productions would be useful.

Try not to be personal in your criticism; your comments should be about what you hear, not about the person who made the programme, so avoid starting sentences with 'What you should have done . . .' or 'You didn't . . .'. Instead try 'I liked . . .', 'I had a problem with . . .', 'I would have liked more/less of . . .' and 'Had you considered . . .?' These sorts of comments and questions should be used as you bear in mind the creative use of the medium which in the case of radio means the contributions made by voices, music and sounds and the quality of these ingredients.

Remember too to think about the listener that the programme is aimed at: you may not be included in that target audience.

What is the story that the programme is trying to tell? Examine the structure of the piece you are listening to; does it tell its story effectively and efficiently? Does it sound as though it has been researched in depth? What sort of contribution does the script and presentation make to the production? Is music used as a bed or illustration – how well does it contribute? Do you get a sense of place or action from the choice and use of actuality sounds? Are the contributors appropriate and authoritative? Consider the interview material; the quality of the questions, if they are included, and of the replies. Then, of course, you should keep an ear on the technical quality of the programme: did you notice any edits, were the sounds well mixed and balanced, was it well recorded? Overall was it a good bit of radio? This activity is also something you will have to take part in if you work in broadcasting so hopefully you will be equipped to comment and feedback on your own work and that of others.

Students, like broadcast professionals, also have to sell their ideas for practical project work to their lecturers, who take on the role of commissioning editors. Again it is worth thinking about how best to convince them that your idea is a good one and that you are capable of bringing a completed programme to fruition. You need to sell yourself and the production, make it relevant and appropriate for a particular audience and justify the format and content of the programme. See it from the commissioning editor's point of view – explain what the programme will sound like and demonstrate that there is substance and research behind the idea by using examples. Finally offer up a brief summary of your proposal and leave them with something to think about.

Radio, like the broadcasting industry overall, is creative, opinionated and evolving. It is regulated and monitored and the output produced subject to ethical and legal considerations. To succeed you need tenacity, skill, talent and imagination. Production techniques and methods of working change only when experienced broadcasters are confident in their abilities and knowledge and are comfortable enough with technology to try something new.

'Those working in the media industry need to be continually developing their skills to keep up with (those) changes and keep us as an industry ahead of the game' (www.skillset.org/research/workforce-survey).

Enjoy your radio listening and your programme making.

1
Broadcasting programmes

In those formative listening years that I mention in the Introduction to this book my family tuned into their favourite programmes on a colourful transistor radio. My grandparents by contrast never progressed beyond their gigantic valve-operated wooden piece of furniture called the wireless. Once it had been switched on and given time to warm up it was permanently tuned to the portentous voices on the Home Service from the BBC. The output of the networks that we chose to listen to seemed to be reflected in our choice of receiving equipment. Our listening routines were also coloured and shaped by the portability of the modern radio that was taken from room to room, into the garden and on days out. The plugged-in valve wireless determined that listening was a sedentary activity.

Although the BBC was at this time the sole UK provider of radio programmes it didn't mean that listeners tuned into their services alone. Disgruntled with the lack of choice that comes with a monopoly and the dull nature of some of the output, especially on Sundays, radio owners were encouraged to tune across the dial in search of more lively English language and music programmes provided particularly by European stations. However, other listeners, afraid that they would never be able to find their original station frequency again, would stay tuned to that station and never touch the retuning dial.

It is worth bearing in mind that any programmes you produce will be heard in the context of the station that broadcasts them and the rest of its output. Programmes combine to form a consistent station identity and style to its schedule that will appeal to a particular audience profile. This identity is reflected in its choice of presenters of the programmes, station name, station jingle package and music choice. Listening to a station or network becomes part of the daily routine and lifestyle choice for some and an audience will make a special effort to tune in regularly attracted by the style of the presenter, the music choice or the content of the programmes. A station's programming policy needs to be established in the mind of the listener as soon as they turn on and everything it broadcasts should match up with that listener's expectations every time they tune in. If they know what they can expect to hear they will come back for more and leave their radios tuned to you when they switch off for the day so that your station will be the one their radio is tuned to when they switch on next morning.

However, there is a danger that consistent format, structure and content can end up being acceptably formulaic and taken up by other stations in a group. The result is a somewhat sanitised and indistinguishable-sounding output when they should be aiming for diversity. Stations need to be able to introduce surprises for their listeners, though not so often or with so strong a surprise that they tune away, and they need to develop strategies to encourage new listeners without alienating their current devotees.

All broadcasters have a picture in their mind of who is their audience. They know their age, have ideas about what they do for a living and in their spare time, what they care about and what they talk about so everything that is broadcast, advertised and marketed is targeted at and angled for them.

Knowing your audience is vital to good programme making, says Katy McDonald of Metro FM:

> *If you can provide something that deliberately appeals to them they will stay with you and even forgive one or two minor imperfections. Your programme could be excellent with quality content, stylish presentation, humour, good music but it will be a flop if it is wrongly targeted.*

Stations that include music therefore need to make sure they are playing tracks that will appeal to that target audience. The music that is seen as the soundtrack to your life will be positioned during your late teens or early twenties. A station in 2006 playing music from the 1970s will see their audience as being in their 40s and 50s. They may also feature contemporary music that has the same appeal and speech content would reflect that audience's interests.

In their bid to establish an identity with their listeners stations will insist on a set way for presenters to identify the station, its frequencies, its address, phone-in number and email details. There will also be set routines and scripts leading up to and out of news bulletins, advert breaks, traffic news and weather. The promotion of the station, its logo and presenters has become more sophisticated over the years with stations producing magazines, web sites and being involved in joint promotions with record companies and event promoters. However, you can still buy station mugs, pens and car stickers or get a free publicity photograph of your favourite presenter.

Listening to radio rather than listening to *the* radio is even more applicable today because radio stations and their programmes can be accessed via a number of means, not just using a specifically designed device called a radio. I have six radios operating in various rooms of my home, one in my car, one at work and one in my jacket pocket. I can also listen via my cellphone, on the Web via my computer or by selecting a station on cable and satellite TV. Radio is no longer as ephemeral as it once was. We no longer need to listen to programmes in real time as they are broadcast: we can record on-air or access a listen again archive on a web site when it is more convenient for us. It is the continued act of listening that is important because the listener is an essential part of the broadcasting equation.

Ed Shane was worried that there would be no listeners to radio in the future, but puts his faith in the Internet generation – he calls them 'screenagers' – who experience radio by listening via their computers (Keith 2002: 187–8). This means that they will be lucky enough to be able to access radio from all over the world and interact with the stations and their presenters, giving them a fuller and more satisfying relationship with the medium than any previous generation of listeners.

Technology has changed and will continue to change the way we listen to radio and also the way it is produced. Don't get the impression all radio stations have the latest high-tech equipment at their disposal: some are a long way from tapeless production. Not all studios are working digitally and lack scheduling and playout systems, digital editing software or memory card recorders. As the BBC in-house newspaper reported, the daily consumer programme *You and Yours* on Radio 4 only became the first factual programme to broadcast 100 per cent digitally in December 2004.

There are still radio departments who are recording programmes, interviews and the like on quarter-inch tape and editing with chinagraph pencils, razor blades and splicing tape. Acquire as many skills as you can with new and not so up-to-date equipment – you never know where you might end up working.

You don't even have to be a professional broadcaster with state of the art studio facilities and transmitters at your disposal to get listeners. Podcasting (named after the popular MP3 player the Ipod made by Apple) enables amateur broadcasters based at home and armed with a computer and microphone to speak to their listeners via downloadable audio files, avoiding the accepted industry method of programme making and transmitting. They are beginning to reach audiences who don't listen to conventional radio because they personally find what is on offer, whether it is music or speech content, unacceptable or not to their taste. Material can be targeted directly for this specialist taste audience. Wise podcasters will also appreciate the potential advertising opportunities designed for and directed at the individual listener. The system is also open to abuse because, unlike the broadcast professionals, the podcasters are not regulated or bound by codes of practice. Professional broadcasters in the UK including the BBC are now starting to experiment with providing certain programmes and programme extracts from their output for downloading to MP3 players. According to Simon Nelson, Controller, BBC Radio and Music Interactive, the BBC's top five monthly downloads for 2005 were the 08.10 interview on Radio 4's *Today* programme, the best of Chris Moyles on Radio 1, the documentary archive on World Service, *From Our Own Correspondent* and *In Our Time* on Radio 4. All these programmes are produced by the BBC in-house programme makers and are all factual speech-based material. This is because the BBC needs to avoid clearance and copyright problems if they made available fictional work, work produced by an independent production company or included music. Another popular download from the BBC was Radio 3's Beethoven season (*2005 The Beethoven Experience*) when the network broadcast all of the composer's works. They were able to make this available for download because the music was out of copyright and all the musicians performing were part of BBC orchestras recorded by BBC staff.

Interactivity between the listener and a programme, broadcaster or station has changed dramatically. Back in the 1960s and earlier the best you could hope for was to send a postcard requesting a record to be played on your favourite show or ask for a dedication to be read out for a birthday, wedding or exam success. Postcards were also the preferred form of contact when entering competitions organised by the station. If you wrote in to a DJ you might be sent a signed photograph to stick on the refrigerator. Later technology enabled phone calls from the listener to be heard on air. Now we are encouraged, if we have the technology, to respond immediately to what we hear in the form of emails or message boards. The number and range of stations available to us in the UK has increased and the Web allows us access to stations all over the world. The listener has always been an extra resource for broadcasters by eliciting contributions from them in the form of information and eye-witness accounts and there has been a move recently to encourage more 'citizen journalism' via mobile phones to feed the immediacy and 24/7 nature of radio news.

Broadcasters in the UK are regulated. Whether you are running an RSL station on a twenty-eight-day licence, broadcasting on a national or local commercial station or are part of the BBC system there is an organisation of people making sure you do it right and making sure you are answerable if you break the law, offend anyone or don't provide what you promised to the listener.

BBC radio, including its national and local services, is funded by a contribution from the TV licence fee. Independent or commercial radio, including national and local stations, is paid for by the advertising and sponsorship they carry. In the USA subscription revenues and sponsorship to radio via satellite services means there is no need for advertisements. Some of the larger BBC regions will split their output during the course of a programme so that more locally focused news and information can be broadcast to smaller audiences, so for example during a breakfast show heard across a large county at certain set times staff in local studios dotted about the area will opt-out of the programme and broadcast a news, travel and information bulletin for their specific audience.

It is possible to access the output of radio stations across the world via the Internet, and this is particularly useful if you want to hear, for example, their particular spin or angle on world news stories. Many listeners like to listen to the radio from their computer at the same time as they surf the net, especially in the evening, using it as a soundtrack and to keep them company. Having access to a station's output, particularly one where you are out of range of their transmitters, is useful should you decide to apply for a post with them – at least you will be able to check out their sound. Prior to this service being available candidates would either have to spend a day in a hotel on the patch monitoring the station on a portable radio or ask someone already working there to send them a recording of some of the programmes and bulletins.

In the UK there has never been as much choice in the range of stations as there has been in other countries, but there is quite a selection of programming choice for general audiences. The gaps show in the poor range of available programmes or services for specialist or minority interests usually broadcast during off-peak listening times and which are more and more being served by web radio stations.

The main BBC services are:

- BBC Radio 1 – New music for a younger audience

- BBC Radio 2 – Popular music, specialist music and light entertainment for a mature audience

- BBC Radio 3 – Classical music plus jazz, world music, arts, drama and experimental features

- BBC Radio 4 – Speech-based new and current affairs, drama, comedy, documentaries and features

- BBC Five Live – 24-hour news and sport

- BBC World Service – Broadcasts music and English-language speech and about 40 other languages aimed at audiences overseas. Note this service is not funded by the UK licence fee but by a grant from the Foreign and Commonwealth Office of the British Government.

The BBC's digital audio broadcasting (DAB) services:

- 1Xtra – Contemporary urban UK music

- BBC Five Live Extra – Live coverage of sports events

- BBC 6 Music – Popular music outside the mainstream

- BBC 7 – Archive comedy, drama and children's programmes

- BBC Asian Network – Music and speech for British Asians.

The BBC also has regional and local services:

- BBC Radio Scotland

- BBC Radio Wales (English language service)

- BBC Radio Ulster

- BBC Radio Cymru (Welsh language service)

- BBC Radio nan Gaidheal (Gaelic language service)

- There are also 30-plus county-wide local stations in England offering local speech and music for local audiences. Examples are BBC Radio Kent, BBC Radio Leeds etc.

Commercial radio in the UK:

- Independent National Radio (INR)

- Classic FM – Popular classical music

- talkSPORT – Sports coverage and analysis and topical debate

- Virgin Radio – Popular and contemporary music.

DAB services

A wide range available around the country depending on your location but include:

- OneWord – Drama, readings and discussion about books

- Planet Rock – Classic and contemporary rock music

- Prime Time Radio – Melodic music from 1940s and 50s to the present day.

Independent Local Radio (ILR)

Over 200 music and local news stations around the UK, but with usually smaller coverage areas than BBC stations, some are owned by radio groups like GCap and Emap and Guardian Media Group.

The numbers will vary from year to year as stations change hands and new contracts are awarded by Ofcom. The stations will have names like 96.4, The Eagle, Spirit FM, Fox FM etc. Ofcom is obliged under a section of the 1990 Broadcasting Act 'to do all it can to secure the provision within the UK of a range and diversity of local radio services'. There is usually plenty of competition for these licences. In 2005, for example, Ofcom's new licence for Manchester attracted 19 bids for a service that has the potential for a million-and-a-half adult listeners. It was won by Xfm (owned by the group Gcap), who will provide a format aimed at a male audience in the age range 15–34 years. Of the thirteen applications for a new licence in the north-east of England advertised in 2005 four offer a diet of rock music, five want to provide easy listening or melodic music and speech mix, one all-speech, one children's programming and two alternative music-based formats. Ten of the bids target older audiences and just three aim to serve younger listeners.

You may also find local community stations covering local news and events. These stations are also authorised by Ofcom licences, are non-profit-making and owned and run mostly by volunteers from the local area. They enable these communities to use radio to develop cultural, education, regeneration, employment and creative projects in their area. Community radio, like hospital radio and student radio, is a great training ground for programme makers. You can listen to RSL and Event radio stations broadcasting for a limited period for example during Freshers' week, an arts festival or agricultural show. They may carry paid advertisements and sponsorship of content such as weather reports and travel news. Some of these stations go on to apply for and win full licences if they experience a good trial period and can find financial backing.

Pirate radio stations have been with us since the mid-1960s. These days rather than transmitting from ships anchored outside UK territorial waters the illegal broadcasts tend to be based on the tops of tower blocks. One of the duties of Ofcom is to investigate and try to clamp down on these stations, whose signals can interfere with those of emergency services and of course licensed broadcasters.

Instead of simply playing background muzak to their customers some of the nationwide chains have taken the idea of radio programme formats and 'broadcast' hosted music programmes into their stores. This obviously helps customers identify with the store branding and the DJs can create an atmosphere conducive to shopping. As well as playing music suitable for their customer profile (just like a radio station has a target listenership) there is the opportunity for product placement, information about special offers and focused advertising campaigns.

As well as listening to live broadcasts of programmes you can access many web sites posted by stations which allow you to listen again within a week of the original transmission; others offer longer-term archives of part or whole programmes.

The days of a radio station being only about the single service that comes out of the speaker are long gone. Radio is already a multimedia industry and the importance of multimedia in building and retaining audiences and in providing new revenue streams can only grow in importance in the future.
(Ofcom 2005a)

While radio is evolving, the majority of listening, even in digital homes is still done via the analogue radio sets (82%).
(BBC Audience Research. FACT issue 7 p. 23 September 2005)

So how do radio stations find out who is listening to their programmes, how many listeners they have, when they listen and for how long? In the UK the National Radio Listening Survey or RAJAR conduct the research on their behalf. Listening diaries are issued to members of the public in the form of booklets in which they record details of which stations they have listened to, where they listened and for how long every time they listen for five minutes or more over the course of a week. The results are then passed on to stations to help them in planning their programming. As you can imagine, there is a great deal of anticipation and tension amongst broadcasters when the RAJAR figures are due to be published and they will be concerned if their station or programme has lost listeners to the competition.

It can be a useful exercise to keep your own listening diary for a week. It could help you decide if you listen to enough radio and if you need to broaden your listening range. Are you one of the growing number of listeners who access radio via the Web and does this offer you more choice of listening? Do you feel that the stations you listen to are serving your needs as a listener? If not, why not? Do you actively seek out stations that will provide you with music and speech that will be of interest to you? If you are interested in a particular kind of music, for example folk music, do you search the listing by genre to find out on which stations you can hear your favourite sounds? Compare your findings with others.

Before you start to think about programme ideas for your station make sure you are aware and up to date with the regulations, legislation and codes of practice that form the regulating of broadcasts and broadcasters. It takes a long time to understand the laws and regulations that control what we can and can't say over the airwaves. These are the must-knows and it is not an exhaustive list. Some are based around law and must be adhered to, others are based around best practice and are accepted and understood by the industry. They are not there to take the enjoyment out of production, but to ensure that programme makers get it right and avoid problems for themselves, their contributors and their station. That essential source of reference and good practice produced by the BBC and based on law and the extensive experience of its staff – *Editorial Guidelines*, formerly known as *Producers' Guidelines* – says that we need this sort of information to 'help us to make sensible calculations about those risks by leaning on the experience of others who have been in similar situations'. *The Ofcom Broadcasting Code* (2005) produced after consultation with broadcasters, viewers and listeners and informed by legislation, sets standards for TV and radio broadcasting. It replaces the six codes of previous regulators. It states that 'Broadcasters may make programmes about any issue they choose, but it is expected that broadcasters will ensure at all times that their programmes comply with the general law as well as the Code' (Ofcom 2005: 7).

Both guides say they are not set in stone but are regularly updated and evolve as broadcast content, methods of broadcasting and audience expectations develop and change.

The NUJ Code of Conduct for journalists is also respected by those involved in speech content. It was designed to help develop and maintain the highest possible standards of professionalism across all the media.

LIBEL

The basic rule here, if you want to avoid losing your broadcasting career and ending up in court charged under the law of defamation, is to think before you speak. Are you about to broadcast something about someone that could damage their reputation? Ask yourself 'Would I like that said of me?'

A libellous statement is one that:

• Causes someone to be shunned or avoided

• Lowers a person in the eyes of right-thinking people

• Damages them in their office, trade or profession

• Holds them up to hatred, ridicule or contempt.

Defamation covers libel and slander – the difference between them being that libel refers to broadcast or published material over a wide area and slander refers to words spoken to a small personal audience. Therefore, radio programmes are covered under libel.

If you are editing an interview for your programme and something you hear said by the interviewer or an interviewee sets the alarm bells ringing in your head refer to a higher authority. A phone call to your editor or station legal advisor could stop a lot of problems all round. Good journalists also keep a copy of *McNae's Essential Law for Journalists* (Greenwood and Welsh 2005) within arm's reach for quick reference.

The defence of innocent dissemination is open to broadcasters of live programmes provided they can prove they had no effective control over remarks made by a contributor – for example something said by a studio guest or a caller to a phone-in programme. You also need to demonstrate that you had taken all reasonable care to ensure the libel could not happen. For example the use of a delay system, use of a profanity key, screening procedures by filtering calls through a selection procedure before putting them to air, briefing speakers on the dangers etc. If you think a libel has been committed during your live programme the presenter should be advised to distance themselves, the programme and the station from the statement immediately. This could involve asking the speaker to consider withdrawing the comment, apologising unreservedly on behalf of the station, changing the subject under discussion and even taking the offender off-air so they are not in a position to do it again either deliberately or accidentally. Just because everyone else is speaking about someone you should avoid doing the same: for example, if the newspapers carry a libellous story and you read out the article on air you are repeating it and therefore creating a fresh libel.

Assuming that it was your station that broadcast the material, that it refers to the aggrieved person and was broadcast without their consent, then if you do find yourself being sued under the law of defamation these are the main defences you may be able to use in court:

- Justification, which means you must be able to convince a jury with evidence that the story or comment is true;

- Fair Comment, which means that what was said is based on facts that can be proved to be true and were made without malice in the public interest;

- Absolute Privilege, which covers parliamentary and court proceedings provided the court case was open to the public and reported accurately at the time. MPs have the right to say whatever they like during debates and proceedings in the House of Commons;

- Qualified Privilege, which covers the reporting of parliamentary proceedings, local authority meetings, tribunals and public meetings. It also includes press conferences and their related press releases relating to these meetings. Again the report must be fair and accurate.

In both cases of privilege the public interest must outweigh individual reputations. It is worth noting that anyone suing you will have to prove that anything you broadcast was defamatory and that it was them you were referring to. However, they do not have to prove that what you said is untrue or that they have been harmed in any way.

COPYRIGHT

Copyright is an element of law relating to intellectual property and covers defined classes of 'works' – literary (basically covers words including song lyrics, recorded spoken word, printed word), dramatic (scripts that are for performance) and musical and artistic works (photographs, sculpture). Copyright limits the copying and use of work without the owner's consent.

Any material you use in your programme that you have not written, composed, illustrated, collected yourself will be subject to the laws of copyright under the Copyright, Designs and Patents Act 1988. So if you want to play some music from a commercially released CD in your collection, music composed and played by a local musician either live or recorded for your programme, an author or actor reading an extract from a novel or autobiography, a short extract from a movie or TV programme or scene from the performance of a play you will be required to obtain copyright clearance. This may simply involve obtaining a licensing agreement from a copyright organisation. All professional radio stations will have negotiated agreements with the various bodies but you need to be clear exactly what you are allowed to play and how you must officially log or register the material you featured so that everyone involved gets their just payments. There are usually specially prepared forms that need to be completed.

You will come across the Performing Rights Society (PRS) who look after the interests of the composers and publishers of music, Phonographic Performance Ltd (PPL) who represent the artists who perform the music on commercial recordings and the Mechanical Copyright Protection Society (MCPS) who administer the broadcast rights of non-commercial library music as well as other rights relating to publishing and recording music. You may have to approach individual copyright owners to obtain permission to use material and this may involve an individually negotiated fee. Work must be in some material form before it can be protected by copyright, but if you make a recording of a live performance you will infringe what is known as non-property rights.

Anyone featuring music on air is required to complete a music reporting form with details of the track title, the composer, the publisher, the label and label number, the title of the CD or LP the track was taken from, the name of the performer and the actual duration of the track as used in the programme (which may not necessarily have been the same as the duration of the track itself).

Exceptions to copyright relate to whether a substantial part of the work has been used and whether the work was used as part of a criticism or review; provided the work is available to the public and the identity of the owner is acknowledged this is called fair dealing. There is also inclusion of work which is incidental to the main subject, but this does not apply to music if it is deliberately included.

If you read extracts from stories that you see in a newspaper or a magazine or web site you should at least attribute your source and not give the impression that you have the information first-hand. Think about how you use gossip stories about celebrities gleaned from the press. Do you want second-hand quotes in your programme? What do they say to the listener about you and your station? Are you certain that the content is not libellous?

Don't be caught out by not adhering to the obligations you have as a broadcaster. Here are some common situations that arise. Think about how you might stand on copyright permissions if you want to do the following:

- Interview the conductor of a touring orchestra and record half a minute of him rehearsing the musicians in a piece by Beethoven to use in your package.

- Illustrate an interview with a composer with extracts from commercially available recordings on CDs of his work performed by a variety of artistes.

- Interview shoppers in a marketplace where a busker is performing pop songs in the background.

- During a live interview with an author persuade them to read the opening paragraph from their latest novel.

If you are unsure about how you stand legally or what you can or cannot do within a programme, it is best to ask your contributors to sign a release form which will at least show in writing that you were aware of your responsibilities and attempted to cover yourself and them.

COURTS AND CRIME

You cannot discuss in your programme any court cases that are active: 'active' means that legal proceedings have begun. The responsibility for finding out if a case is underway lies with the broadcaster. You need to check with the police to find out if an arrest warrant has been issued, an arrest has been made or if a person has been charged either in writing or verbally. If so then the case is active and reporting restrictions come into effect limiting exactly what can be reported on air. There must be no discussion on air of any kind – between presenters or with callers on the line – until the person is sentenced or acquitted or the case is discontinued. Remember it becomes active again if an application for appeal is granted. Once the case re-opens the same rules apply. Only exact and accurate reporting of what was said in court can be broadcast unless the judge says otherwise. If a station broadcasts anything that could influence a case then it will be guilty of contempt of court.

The use of recording equipment in court also constitutes contempt (Contempt of Court Act 1981) so if you think you will be attending court regularly to report on proceedings then it might be a good idea to learn shorthand. You will need to be beyond the confines of the court before you can start recording your voice piece so leave your recorder locked in the boot of your car or make arrangements in advance to see if you can leave it with a court official.

The law states that there should be anonymity for life for the victims of sexual offences. It is therefore an offence to broadcast any material which could reveal the victim's identity from the moment they report the offence. There are calls for the law to include anonymity for those accused of the offence at least until they are charged. In the case of offences against children care must be taken not to broadcast anything that could lead to anyone being able to identify the child and that includes naming the school they attend. It is worth noting that anti-social behaviour orders (ASBOs) are imposed by magistrates in a civil law capacity not criminal law, so under 18s can be identified. If a juvenile breaches the order they will be taken to appear before a youth court under a criminal offence and therefore cannot be named.

TASTE AND DECENCY

There is no official 9 pm watershed on radio as there is on television. If a programme contains material that may offend a family audience or discusses adult topics a producer has to use their discretion. Difficulties can arise if material is broadcast during school holidays or other times when children are likely to be listening. A careful eye needs to be kept on any material that is likely to be repeated at a different time of day to the original broadcast.

Descriptions of violence can be just as upsetting to listeners as seeing scenes on TV especially if any audio used, like sounds or actuality, is particularly evocative.

Swearing is usually a demonstration of an individual's lack of word power and inability to communicate effectively. Use of bad language will alienate your audience. Make it a ground rule that neither presenters nor contributors will be allowed to use strong language on air. Look carefully at the words you use in your everyday speech and decide if they would be acceptable on air. Think before you speak especially in the heat of a discussion or during a relaxed chat, as you may slip up in either situation.

If there is an accidental slip of the tongue don't just laugh it off, apologise to the listener and move on quickly. If you think that there is a likelihood that one of your guests will swear on air think about pre-recording their contribution so that you have the option to edit the recording and avoid embarrassment all round.

What you say and the way that you say it on air needs to be considered inoffensive to a general audience. Watch out for innuendo, near the knuckle jokes, etc. unless you want to receive complaints. Opinion about what is tasteful and what can be deemed as decent on radio is divided and broadcasters will sometimes try to stretch the boundaries.

On air comments made by presenters or contributors that are racist, sexist or blasphemous or any bigoted remarks about any person's religious beliefs or sexual orientation should not be tolerated, indeed they may be breaking the law.

DIVERSITY AND PORTRAYAL

It is important that all aspects of society are given fair representation on air. It makes the content of a programme more inclusive and broadens the audience appeal. Encourage diversity by examining your contacts book and seeking a wider range of contributors to represent the views and viewpoints of society. You may even want to share or gather contacts from others you work with. This could help you avoid any preconceptions you may inadvertently bring to your selection of contributors. Casting out a net to find someone new is obviously more time-consuming and risky. When you are under pressure it can be tempting to fall back on your old faithfuls, but make an exception every now and then. Try to find new expertise and unheard voices. When approaching organisations for spokespersons prepared to contribute on air ask them to consider whether they can provide someone other than the usual suspects who may have 'contributing to the media' as part of their job description. It is really the people who have become empowered through their personal experiences that you should be seeking out to contribute. The parents who have to look after a problem child may be preferable to the chairperson of a support organisation if you want someone to talk about how it affects their lives, but not necessarily if your piece is about how funding is spent.

How people are represented on air is important and how we tell their stories can make a difference to how they are perceived generally. Over the years how we cover a person's race, gender, age, sexuality and disability or the issues that affect them has changed for the better. Our understanding of how media coverage and our choice of words can lead to discrimination and marginalisation has grown. Broadcasting organisations, trade unions and support charities through guidelines, training and publications are helping to raise awareness amongst journalists and programme makers thus ensuring that people's views, arguments and issues are covered honestly and fairly.

The NUJ, for example, provides advice leaflets on a wide range of issues and how best to report them.

In its campaigning report *Stop Press!* Scope, a national disability organisation whose focus is people with cerebral palsy, suggests that we should avoid passive victim words in our reporting and use words that respect disabled people as individuals with control over their own lives. For example use terms like non-disabled rather than able-bodied and wheelchair user instead of wheelchair-bound or confined to a wheelchair.

Mind Out for Mental Health published *Mindshift* – a guide to open-minded media coverage of mental health in which they remind us that people with personal experience of mental health problems and mental health services are increasingly willing and empowered to speak to the media. (Mind out for Mental Health: 13) (Available from them at Freepost LON15335, London SE1 1BR.)

The BBC's *Editorial Guidelines* advises programme makers that when describing different groups a good rule of thumb is to ask how people describe themselves.

Organisations like the Women's Radio Group based in London and projects like Women's Hands and Voices in the USA are campaigning to get more women working in and talking on radio. On the web site of the latter they provide what they call a *Toolkit for Anti-Oppression Programming*.

PRIVACY

According to the European Convention on Human Rights we all have a right to privacy. It also says that this right is balanced against the media's right to freedom of expression in the public interest. Since its introduction into UK law in 2000 broadcast media has introduced further guidelines to avoid court cases that could grant injunctions to halt material being transmitted. Broadcasters are now obliged to been seen and heard to treat people fairly, to operate openly and justify any intrusions into someone's private life. This does not mean that journalists will no longer be able to investigate corruption, negligence or criminal activity using secret recording equipment; however, they will be obliged to obtain permission to do so. They will need to show that an open approach will not be appropriate and the recording would be necessary to gather the evidence they need.

Reporters also on occasion accompany officers from public authorities and services when they carry out a raid on private property. Usually the reporter should get approval prior to going along and get consent from the occupier to use the recording as there are legal issues of trespass and consent to be considered; obviously consent may be waived if the raid uncovers illegal activities.

Reporters covering incidents like disasters or accidents should respect privacy by ensuring that they do not intrude into a person's distress or suffering.

Be aware that children have additional rights. Written permission must be obtained before interviewing them and the interview must always be carried out in the presence of a parent or guardian.

ELECTIONS

Unlike newspapers radio stations must not demonstrate any political favour or bias.

Programmes that include coverage of elections are obliged to be fair, balanced and accurate. Extra care needs to be taken to ensure that undue prominence is not given to any one candidate over time during the campaign period and due weight given to all the main parties in any reports or debates.

Once the polls open for general, European or local elections there is very little that broadcasters can say or talk about until the polling stations close. During election day you can only really talk about whether polling has been brisk or slow, the effect that the weather may have on turnout (but not that it will benefit one party rather than another) and the names and parties of the candidates. There must be no mention of opinion polls or predictions about the poll outcome.

Take care during music programmes. The request for 'a piece of music for all the team working hard at the People's Party headquarters' might just slip through the net. Candidates and their supporters should be kept off the airwaves on this day and this includes your top breakfast presenter if they are up for election.

It is a good idea to keep an election log during the pending period (from the day the election is announced until the polls close) so that you can keep track of your coverage to ensure that it is balanced and it can then be used as proof in case of argument.

OBITUARY PROCEDURES

If a major news story breaks a radio station may decide to suspend its usual programme and offer coverage of the story as it develops, a tribute programme or continuous solemn or instrumental music with frequent announcements of the news. When certain members of the British royal family die radio stations have to follow laid down procedures which cover how the news should be announced, what should be on air after the announcement, how often the announcement should be made and what changes will need to be made to subsequent output. Stations around the country are informed by their main source of international and national news: IRN for ILR stations and the General News Service (GNS) for the BBC local stations. Both news organisations will provide official news bulletins followed by the national anthem. No announcement will be made on air until a member of the management team has been informed of the news and no reports will be allowed to go to air unchecked by the News Editor. Pre-prepared tribute programmes, which are updated regularly, will be broadcast. They include regular messages informing listeners about what has happened and why normal programming has been changed. Stations have a list of telephone numbers of potential contributors who have agreed to be called and interviewed for their reaction and share their memories of the deceased. Stations also have collections of music tracks – some solemn, others slow melodic instrumentals that can replace the usual output during the period following the announcements and between special programmes.

The obituary procedure for both the BBC and Independent stations applies in the event of the death of:

- The Queen
- The Prince of Wales
- Prince William
- Prince Harry
- The Duke of Edinburgh
- The Princess Royal

The BBC has what it calls a Category 1 list which means if a senior member of the royal family dies then their local services must join their colleagues in London for the announcement and some subsequent programmes.

Stations will need to consider the mood of their audience and the identity of the deceased to inform the decisions about the degree to which output will need to be altered. Commercial stations will have the extra challenge of having to decide if they should suspend playing adverts.

If you are ever likely to be the only member of staff on duty at the station then you need to make yourself aware of the 'obit procedures', where to find the management contact numbers and know where the recordings for broadcast are stored and how to access them. IRN and the BBC have facilities to give obit warnings to their stations so that they can be prepared before the official announcement from Buckingham Palace is broadcast.

RISK ASSESSMENT

It is not only employers who are responsible for health and safety issues at work: employees are also expected to take reasonable care of their own and others' well-being. If station staff are encouraged to raise and discuss health and safety issues together with appropriate and relevant ongoing training then there will be a heightened awareness of what could happen on, say, a location recording which will lead to more thorough preparation to avoid problems.

The producer of a programme should assess if there are any likely risks as early as possible in the production process. This assessment should be recorded on paper and dated. Most stations will have a pro forma that requires completion and subsequent discussion if risks are identified.

No programme is worth injury or worse to anyone participating in or simply observing the production process. Risk assessment will be minimal for a studio-based programme but is an essential part of the planning stages especially if it involves location contributions or an outside broadcast. Assessing any risks to your production team, anyone working with you from outside the team, contributors and members of the general public who may simply be observing the activity must be carried out simply because risks can be the reason why it is decided to drop a programme idea.

Stations will have their own specially designed forms that must be completed and these will help you to assess any potential risks and decide what action you may need to take to safeguard everyone.

Some situations will lend themselves to common-sense protection – making sure you don't block pavements or obscuring views when conducting vox-pops, wearing reflective clothing and hard hats at roadsides and building sites. What about coverage of a protest march or demonstration? You need to think a little bit more about your strategy at such an event. Will your presence prolong or intensify the event or change people's behaviour? If you follow protesters onto private property will you be accused of trespass? Should you ask protesters to shout slogans so that you can record them for your report? What should you do if protesters start throwing stones etc.?

In some cases it is also worth considering completing a further assessment exercise if the programme format, content or staffing changes during production.

2
The programme-making team

Modern digital production facilities mean that all those involved in a production can listen to their audio and read text material at any time on their own computer, making the communication within the team more efficient and the process more flexible in terms of time management and multi-tasking. Programme making can now in theory be paperless and tapeless. Programme makers also have to consider that the material they use needs to be devised for multi-platform purposes, not simply for radio broadcasting. Marketing the programme via a showpage on the station's web site is also usually their responsibility.

Technology is only part of the story: radio programme making requires human resources. The majority of the budget allocated to fund BBC radio is spent on staffing. The personnel involved in the making of programmes were collectively known as 'production effort' but are now more often referred to as teams or crews. It is possible for one person to produce a complete programme, while others are made by small or large teams. The staffing that makes up these teams varies depending on the content and structure of individual programmes, if they are being produced by an independent production company and the size and nature of the station that broadcasts the programme.

Even within the same organisation there can be a variety of working methods. For example when John Ryan (currently Managing Editor at GMR [Greater Manchester Radio]) took over as manager of BBC Radio Leeds he took the radical step of changing the traditional way programme staff worked on the output of the station. As is common practice on many stations the staff were in programme groups working solely to their slice or island of the daily schedule, for example the mid-morning or drivetime slots. In order to give the programme staff a new momentum and encourage new approaches to working routines and thinking John simply divided the staff into two groups. One group worked on today's output and breaking stories while the other group work on material for tomorrow onwards. So everyone got to contribute to planning, fixing interviews, pre-recording items, devising themed material, campaigns etc., thus allowing them to discover and demonstrate hidden talents and learn new skills while still making use of their accumulated knowledge.

More often than not working in teams tends towards the hierarchical rather than the equal. It should be possible, if there is trust in ability and acknowledgement of an individual's contribution regardless of their official post or job description, for a programme to be made by a linked chain circle of people's interdependent skills, rather than from the pyramid structure so often seen as the model of operations. This culture of mutual support and encouragement should be present at all levels of production. The relationship that develops between people working on the same programme is very important. As a programme maker with the BBC Fran Acheson won three Sony awards. She points out that the little things mean a lot.

'When a presenter you like says "it would be really nice to work with you again", that's always a huge compliment.' She also has ideas about supporting members of your team:

> I think it is important to consider where each member of your team wants to be in five years time and helping them to develop the skills you want them to have now to do their job and also what they will need to help them move forward. Jobs are no longer for life and the radio world is more fluid than ever before.

Katy McDonald, who began her radio career as a technical operator, moved into sports reporting and is now a news reporter for Metro FM and Magic in north-east England, offers this advice for anyone hoping to join a radio programme team:

> Be enthusiastic and take every opportunity offered. There are so many chances to do amazing things in this industry but they only come your way if people think you are up for it. In many cases the money isn't great but we do it because we're passionate and want to make the most out of it. And never say you're using radio as a stepping stone to TV – they hate that.

At one time those who worked in radio usually had a specific role or specialism and this still applies in some areas of production and journalism. Many staff are required to be multi-skilled and involved in the programme-making process from initial research, fixing contributors, interviewing and editing material.

Generally anyone involved in radio programme production should have good communication skills that enable them to talk with other staff at different levels, the general public and contributors who could be politicians, celebrities etc. plus a good general knowledge and awareness of current affairs involving people, places and issues. Above all they need the ability and passion to listen to advice, to other's stories and to the radio.

A small word of warning, based on personal experience and the experience of others: you will probably never be told you are doing a good job. It is expected that you will do a good job – after all, that is why you were chosen to do it and what you are paid for. However, if you don't come up to scratch you will be told as much. Whatever the task you will also probably be thrown in at the deep end. If you manage to struggle through and survive someone will take credit for discovering you, if you sink then it will be seen as your own fault. So if you have any doubts about any aspect of the work you are given to do don't be afraid to ask someone in the know. If you are asked to do something that you feel is beyond your present capabilities then make some enquiries about possible training opportunities on offer and discuss it with your supervisor.

Anyone working in radio should master some basic skills to make them more employable and useful. These include writing for radio (writing scripts and information that will be read aloud), a knowledge of the law as it affects broadcasters, interviewing in both live and recorded situations, audio editing and mixing.

It is also important that anyone working in radio has good team-working skills, an ability to work to deadlines and manage their time, an ability to think and act quickly, flexibility, creative ability to develop and deliver ideas, IT skills and a varied and up-to-date contacts book.

Everyone starting a new job or task wonders how much time they should be spending on it. How long should it take to edit this interview or how much time should I spend on this research? Be guided by whoever asks you to do the task – simply ask. The more experienced you become, particularly at something like editing, the faster and more accurate and efficient you become. The important thing is to meet the deadline, especially if what you are doing is directly connected to a programme for broadcast. Time management is all about organisation: pay attention to little things like making sure you have a pen and pad ready when you answer the phone and knowing exactly what you want to say when you call someone can all help.

The Radio Academy web site contains a useful section entitled *Getting into Radio* where you can hear professionals giving advice about journalism, presentation, production and engineering.

Some people make a career working solely in local radio; others see it as a step towards national recognition in radio or television. Some take staff posts but over a quarter accept freelance contracts. You will find freelance presenters on some stations who 'show and go' – in other words they present their programme and then spend the rest of the day working elsewhere – and journalists who will come in for a news reporting or newsreading shift.

There is no consistency in the choice of job titles in broadcasting. The BBC has its range and commercial radio, although adopting some of the same, also have their own preferences. Titles do change with fashion and as multi-skilling demands taking on other or alternative duties. What we can explore are the roles, responsibilities, qualifications and qualities of the people directly involved in programme making. Anyone working in radio programme making will have transferable skills – organising, IT operations, team-leading, supervising etc., but there are also specialist skills that are related solely to their jobs as part of the production team – writing, presenting, interviewing, editing, reporting and operating technical equipment.

MANAGING EDITOR/EDITOR

Generally you need someone to take overall responsibility for the running of a station, a senior figure who can be consulted over policy and legal decisions. They are not perhaps involved in the day-to-day duties of programme production but are major contributors to the scheduling and style of the output.

PROGRAMME CONTROLLER (ILR AND INR)/ PROGRAMME EDITOR (BBC LOCAL)

This post performs a management role, but with a hands-on brief to oversee the programme output of a station, to recruit and supervise on-air talent and to be responsible for the promotion of the station in the community. Many who hold this post will have been promoted from the ranks of senior journalists and programme producers.

NEWS EDITOR

As well as running the newsroom, overseeing bulletins, organising use of staff and resources the news editor will often contribute guidance and advice to programmes and programme teams. This ranges from initial legal pointers to suggesting how a news item could be moved on and developed into programme material like interviews, discussions, outside broadcasts, phone-ins etc.

This is particularly applicable to the role of the news editor of an independent radio station. As well as regular bulletins stations will often have three longer news programmes at the listening peak times throughout the day – one as part of the breakfast show, the next at lunchtime and the last during the drivetime programme in the early evening.

Caroline Kingsmill is News Editor at Spirit FM in Chichester, West Sussex. This is a typical day for her.

04.45   Alarm goes off.
05.15   Arrive at radio station. Check news wires, monitor TV news channels and

check teletext. Make calls to local police, coastguard and fire service to find out if they were called out to any significant shouts overnight.

05.30 Take IRN audio cuts and print off information about stories likely to be covered by them that day. Check stories and other material left as 'overnights' and prepare material for news programme.

06.00 Present news programme – 15 minutes of news, business information and sport.

06.30 Read news and sport headlines.

06.40 Take new IRN audio cuts and prepare bulletin.

07.00 Read four minute bulletin.

07.20 Update station web site with main stories.

08.00 Read four minute bulletin.

08.10 Start planning rest of the day's news output, what stories need developing and make list of potential interviewees to call after 9 am.

08.30 Read news and sport headlines.

08.40 Take IRN audio cuts and prepare bulletin material.

09.00 Read three minute bulletin.

09.05 Start fixing interviews.

09.40 Take IRN cuts and prepare bulletin material.

10.00 Read three minute bulletin.

10.05 Brief day journalist about ongoing local stories, who we are chasing for interview etc. They'll prepare and read bulletins and news programmes until 2 pm and conduct phone and studio interviews. I concentrate on getting more stories.

10.15 Drive to Goodwood motor circuit for a press launch of their Revival Weekend to record interviews with drivers taking part in a celebration 1950s race.

11.30 Head back to office. Stop off to conduct second interview with a career adviser about new scheme to support young people.

12.00 Load interview material into editing system to be cut later.

12.30 Make sure journalists are happy with the day's stories, chase up further interviewees, rewrite some stories and take news cuts from recorded interviews.

13.15 Drive home. Eat and sleep.

17.30 Wake up.

18.30 Meet friends who have just finished work for drinks.

22.00 Go to bed. Set alarm for 04.45.

HEAD OF OUTPUT/HEAD OF SPEECH/HEAD OF MUSIC

These self-explanatory post titles began in ILR but are gradually being introduced to BBC local stations. They are primarily hands-on supervisory roles to assist in the overall coordination of the two main contribution areas of programming. The people who do these jobs will probably be experienced programme makers in their own right.

PRESENTER

A presenter fronts the overall programme at the microphone. It is a performance. They speak directly to the listener from a prepared script or notes that they may alter to suit their style of delivery or through improvised speech. They may also be required to carry out interviews during the programme and operate studio equipment during the broadcast. This is an important role as it is the one most directly linked to communicating with the listener. Presenters are therefore not only the voice but also the face of a radio station, according to Shingler and Wieringa (1998). They reflect the personality, philosophy and image of the station to the audience and so must be chosen carefully. Some stations, particularly those who broadcast mostly sequence programmes, use presenters as continuity announcers to link the programmes together, to give the whole a sense of identity and help keep the flow of the output going. They should also have good presentation skills, be able to take control of the output and if necessary fill in or even take over if there is a break in the broadcast. A programme can be enhanced and deemed a success with a good presenter, but can be let down, even if the content is excellent, by a weak one. A good presenter sounds relaxed, authorative and natural. They need to be able to express their personality through their voice and on-air presence and have the confidence of the listener that they will represent them and their concerns when interviewing. They need the skills and talent to keep their programme popular with the listener.

Some programmes employ two presenters to work together presenting the same programme. This is known as double-heading. On Capital Radio Chris Tarrant used to be paired with Howard Hughes. Both had a specific role – Tarrant was the main presenter and Hughes the newsroom associate. This was particularly useful when the programme had to move from light to serious or vice versa. This doesn't mean that Tarrant could not cover hard news or Hughes make a joke, it was just that you needed Tarrant to be on air while Hughes kept an eye and ear on developing news stories which he fed into the programme.

Listeners also like to hear a balance of voices through the use of a male and female double-header. The roles can be further extended into a 'broadcasting relationship'.

We have had real life husband and wife teams in the past but there is nothing wrong with artificially creating an on-air role for the presenters where they might sound like a listener's favourite auntie full of anecdotes and good advice or a bright nephew who knows all about the latest mobile phones etc. However, I do think we are past the stage where stations provided presenters who were supposed to be perceived as husband or boyfriend substitutes for lonely housewives.

Other stations like the 'zoo' format where the main presenter reacts with a studio full of sidekicks who also make specific contributions to the programme content. This, according to Hendy (2000: 75), means that the voice of the individual presenter can be absorbed into the overall sound that is produced as they bounce and feed off each other.

Whatever the role or personality of the presenter the listener expects them to be sincere, technically competent and professional. As well as putting across your personality on air you will reveal aspects of your life outside the studio to the listener. This is all part of building a relationship with them. Your friendly voice on air and the warm personality you demonstrate at personal appearances or station events can give some people the impression that you must be their friend. You may find the occasional listener who is always trying to speak to you during the phone-in or emailing you everyday or even sending small gifts to get your attention. Be careful not to give too much away. If listeners find out where you live then they will arrive unexpectedly on your doorstep. Letting slip that your flat is empty all day when you are abroad on holiday can lead to you becoming a victim of crime. Also be aware of the impression you are creating if, when you try to establish your credibility, you start bragging about how much you had to drink at the weekend or other behaviour that could be seen as promoting or encouraging others to follow suit.

Your best friend or your worst enemy during the programme making process is your working relationship with your production team – especially the producer/studio producer. Don't get a reputation for being an awkward or difficult person to work with. Yes have your standards and demands, but develop good communication skills with these people and remember that they rely on you as much as you rely on them. After all, you all want the programme to be acclaimed and even award-winning!

If you feel experienced enough make programme suggestions during production meetings. Praise a job well done – a helpful research brief with thoughtful questions included that made you sound good on air for example – and at the end of the programme or recording thank all concerned.

Think about your favourite presenter. Ask yourself why you like them. Is it the sound of their voice? Is it what they say and the way they say it to you? Is it their knowledge of the music they play or the incisive way they conduct an interview or their sparkling wit? Listen to other presenters and compare their different qualities. What role do you think they are playing on air – do you think of them as a parental figure, spouse, sibling, older or younger relation?

PRODUCER

A producer is a team leader who has overall responsibility to coordinate the programme, strand or series content and staffing. They will need to be experienced and creative enough to develop an idea and see it through to broadcast. The producer is the linchpin in radio programme making as they are the overseer, ideas person, researcher, planner, editor, supervisor and director.

This advertisement, which appeared in *The Radio Magazine* in July 2005, is typical.

> *London's Heart 106.2 is looking for an experienced producer, bursting with ideas and creativity, to work on 'Heart Breakfast with Jamie Theakston'.*
> *The main responsibility is to produce world-class breakfast programming as part of a lively, dynamic and talented team.*
> *If you want to apply you will need to have top quality creative skills, first-class technical skills (including desk driving and digital editing). Great energy and enthusiasm. A passion for breakfast radio. Flexibilty in lifestyle and skill set.*

The relationship between producer and presenter is a special one that needs to be nurtured in an atmosphere of trust and for the good of the programme. Sometimes friction can occur for a number of reasons. The presenter may feel they are more experienced than the producer and assert that they know best what is required of their performance. It could be that the producer may not be diplomatic or supportive enough when giving feedback or constructive criticism to the presenter. Whatever happens you must be professional and both be aiming for the best result possible for all concerned in the programme production process. Anyone who has experienced working from both sides of the microphone will tell you that communication is the most difficult part of the job – which is ironic when you think about it as they are both working in the communication industry.

So how can you improve the working relationship between the producer and the presenter?

- Keep the presenter in touch with all developments relating to their contribution to the programme.

- Get relevant programme material such as running order, scripts and research notes to them in good time.

- Brief them efficiently on how you hear the overall programme and their contribution to it in your head.

- Listen to their suggestions and ideas for the programme or their contribution to it.

STUDIO PRODUCER

A studio producer is in charge of the programme as it is being broadcast or recorded in the studio: they ensure that the programme as decided by the producer is made as designed and runs to time. This role is often carried out by the producer. Studio production can also include directing the presenter during transmission or recording. Here are a few simple guidelines to help you get the best out of the presenter:

- Allow time for rehearsal, even if you are involved in regular programmes. You should at least rehearse the opening and closing sequences, particularly if you have a complex menu sequence with taster clips and music beds at the start.

- Give regular feedback during rehearsal and during the programme.

- For most of the time you will be in the cubicle area with your presenter in the studio and communication will be via talkback. Presenters can feel very isolated if you don't keep them in touch with what is going on. Tell them you are ignoring them because you need to sort out the links to the guest in the satellite studio or you are thinking of changing the running order or you can't find the piece of music to start the programme. This way they won't feel left out or concerned that you are talking about them.

- During the programme let them get on with their job of entertaining the listener. Keep your communication with them to a minimum by using the talkback sparingly and calmly even if everything is falling apart on your side of the glass. If necessary talk to them at a time when it is less likely to spoil their concentration, for example, when a music track is playing.

- Make eye contact and give a few reassuring smiles or thumbs-up as required.

- Always thank the presenter and the rest of the studio team for a job well done.

You will also be responsible for making sure all the programme material is available in the studio prior to broadcast and supervise the studio manager/technical operator during the programme.

STUDIO MANAGER (BBC NATIONAL AND WORLD SERVICE)

The studio managers (usually abbreviated to SM) set up and operate studio equipment for and during a programme under the direction of the studio producer or a senior SM. They can usually solve any technical problems and contribute ideas about the best way to achieve complicated mixes. They will also contribute to the editing of a recorded programme.

ENGINEER

The engineer on a radio station is obviously responsible for the installation and maintenance of all broadcast equipment and supervision of technical staff. They should also play an integral part in the planning and staging of any outside broadcast or station event. They will try out and recommend new equipment and software to be used as part of station production and broadcast.

TECHNICAL OPERATOR (ILR)

The 'tech op' is the commercial radio equivalent of the SM and is called on to operate studio and location equipment for the programme makers, particularly during a complex production or outside broadcast. You will be working to tight deadlines and need to stay calm under pressure.

Don't leave anything to chance. Make sure everything is working properly before the start of a broadcast or recording. You will have enough to cope with once the programme is rolling without having to deal with things that should and could have been sorted earlier. Remember to take sound levels efficiently and check for quality of sound too. Are there enough microphones and headphones?

PRODUCTION/BROADCAST ASSISTANT (PA/BA)

This is perhaps the most difficult post to define clearly as all production teams will have different needs. Suffice to say you can expect to be an important part of a production team and, along with the producer, you will have a clear overall view of the programme as you will be involved at every stage. This is a coordinating and support role covering most activities from basic research, fixing arrangements for travel and other logistic requirements like ordering up music and archive recordings, booking studios and ISDN lines, hospitality, preparing documentation like running orders, scripts, music logs, programme as broadcast (PasBs) etc. under the supervision of the producer.

RESEARCHER

Research is ongoing throughout the programme making process and is carried out by all staff involved. However, a specific researcher is required to establish background, biographical and historical facts about a topic or guest interviewee. This will certainly involve initial over-the-phone interviews with the guest. You will be expected to have and maintain a comprehensive contacts book. There may also be a requirement for sources of other audio material like music, archive or sound effects which you need to be able to source. Researchers will often be called upon to prepare research briefs, questions and notes about interviewees etc. for producers and presenters. (See chapter 4, *Making programmes*, for details of what a brief should contain.) A good researcher will have an eye and ear for detail, good interviewing skills and knowledge of sources of information, organisations, spokespersons and experts.

REPORTER

The number of reporters or journalists working in the newsroom and on programmes will depend on the size of the station, whether it is BBC, INR or ILR, the patch it covers, its budget and its commitment to local news coverage. On commercial stations, for example, the presenters and the advertising and promotions staff generate income for the station and so earn their keep: news and speech programming costs money. Across the board you may find a solitary reporter at one station and a team of half a dozen at another. Reporters are expected to provide the news coverage for a station by actively searching out local news and reacting to international and national stories. The news producer who is 'on the desk' for a particular shift will usually be the person responsible for allocating reporters to cover particular stories. A programme may also have a reporter role to feed in stories or go out and about while the presenter is studio based.

Reporters need to be inquisitive, persistent, have good communication skills and a good knowledge of the law, public affairs and current affairs.

Even the listener can cast themselves in the role of reporter. By encouraging inter-activity radio stations now receive regular calls from listeners stuck in traffic jams updating the information and news being broadcast by the station as eyewitnesses to events. Incidentally, travel reporters and the like always check any information from callers with a motoring organisation, council or police prior to broadcast to confirm the facts, but always attribute the caller. Obviously because the caller is on the scene it is possible that they are the first to be aware of delays or incidents before the authorities.

Audience-generated content is making an increasingly important contribution to breaking news stories like the effects of extreme weather, terrorist incidents, sieges, hijacks and accidents. This is useful to help give a full picture of an event or incident, but it does put extra pressure on the professional broadcasters to ensure that any comments broadcast are within legal guidelines and will not jeopardise any related future court cases.

CORRESPONDENT

More often in a BBC post the correspondent is a specialist reporter who will cover stories related to their particular area such as politics, education, or arts when they are in the news. Correspondents are also required to provide background and historical context to stories on air and for research purposes. Their contacts book should read like a who's who of those involved in their subject area and include home and personal mobile phone numbers of the great and good. They should not only be able to recognise the important players but also be recognised by them in turn. This relationship can be particularly useful at press conferences, media briefings, media scrum interviews and at times like weekends when people are often difficult to get hold of, let alone be prepared to make a contribution to a programme or interview. Like reporters they will use a range of modes of delivery to present their stories but the live two-way is usually the favoured method, especially in news or topical coverage.

The BBC also has a number of foreign or overseas correspondents who report on stories in their part of the world. A local contact who feeds information and reports when called upon is known as a 'stringer'.

The BBC has a long-running programme called *From Our Own Correspondent* in which correspondents based overseas are asked to provide a dispatch in the form of a voice piece about life in their particular region or how living and working in that part of the world is impacting on them. There have been many thoughtful, touching and humorous contributions over the years, but because these are usually personal albeit professional insights, they can sometimes be controversial. Barbara Plett sparked complaints when she filed a dispatch from Palestine and described how she started crying when she saw a helicopter carrying a frail Yasser Arafat to hospital. The BBC originally ruled that the report did not breach their impartiality guideline, but this decision was later overruled by the corporation's governors.

BROADCAST JOURNALIST (BJ)

The BJ, like the reporter and the news producer, will be based in the newsroom of a station. However, they are more likely to be involved in feeding material to programmes for development and comment. Senior to the reporter and more experienced, the BJ will also be expected to be able to contribute to news in other areas such as TV and online.

INTERVIEWEES

You report the news or tell a story, but interviewees are the people who *are* the news or the story. It is their experiences, feelings and opinions that make up the content of programmes. Referred to as contributors or interviewees by the programme team, but more often simply the guests, they are the most unpredictable ingredient of your programme. They will not be working from a prepared script: to get the best out of them brief them and make as much fuss of them as you would the presenter.

They, like you, will need to research and prepare themselves for the contribution they will be making so brief them and answer any questions they may have for you.

Explain why you want them particularly to appear on your programme. This gives them the opportunity to explain why they may not be the right person and suggest an alternative, or they can show off their knowledge and communications skills to confirm your intitial expectations of them.

Outline in general terms what you expect their contribution to be in the programme, but not the specific questions they may be asked during the course of it.

Explain the nature of the programme they will be appearing in and who will be talking to them on air. If there is time suggest they listen to an edition of the programme so they can get a feel for it.

Make sure they understand the station and audience profile – they may not be listeners or they may need to adjust the wording or style of speech to communicate better with the listener. For example a scientist or academic used to pitching explanations to their peers may need to think about whether their usual use of language and jargon will be appropriate for a radio programme aimed at youngsters.

Give them full details of where, when and for how long their live or recorded contribution will be. They will probably ask you who else will be taking part in their segment of the programme, especially if that person holds contrary views to them. You should volunteer this information anyway, especially if there is to be a phone-in element which may involve them in answering questions or arguing points with listeners who call in.

Remember to ask them to arrive in good time and if they don't have a mobile phone number to give you make sure they have the studio number so if they get held up they can call and warn you. Make sure there is someone available to meet and greet them and show them to the studio.

Before they enter the studio ask them to leave their mobile phone outside – after all you don't want it going off during the programme. Explain the studio procedures such as how close they should be in front of the microphone, what a red light means, to stay quietly seated after their contribution etc.

REGULAR CONTRIBUTORS

Other voices that will add to your programme mix will come from the staff at weather and travel (road, rail, air and ferry) organisations with the latest updates and information. Usually they will know exactly what is expected of them, but if you ever start feeling that information is not being communicated effectively for the listener then talk to them about how the system could be improved. It is also interesting to note that presenters will often indulge in a bit of banter with a travel or weather contributor so they need to be confident with their on-air persona. Incidentally, banter between a presenter and newsreader before, during or after a bulletin, particularly if it involves discussion about one of the stories, is usually frowned upon.

Some programmes like to have regular slots for guest experts who become well known to the listeners. This may include a monthly visit to the studio by a vet, consumer expert, film reviewer etc. You should always discuss the subject area with them well in advance to give them a chance to research. Encourage them to make suggestions about the topic you could discuss. Make sure they stay focused on it during the broadcast and always give them honest regular feedback about their contribution. A time may come when you have to drop them from the programme because of budget constraints or a scheduling shake-up. A professional approach to the relationship will help you let them down gently so warn them when they start that it might not be forever.

Many stations have a help or action desk manned by someone employed by a social action charity to act as coordinator. They can make useful on-air contributions with simple appeals from individuals or local charity or support groups or dissemination of advice and information in a regular scheduled slot. They will also get involved in any charity or social action campaigns run by the station.

3
The programme

The listings magazine *Radio Times* was first published in September 1923. Reading through early editions you can't help but notice that the output of the BBC services at that time was made up of individual one-off items standing in isolation. These initial broadcasts were not regular daily or weekly slots so not seen as programmes that would attract and hold or build an audience and persuade them to make an appointment to listen at a set time. At some point in the BBC's history someone must have made a conscious decision that it would be a good idea to broadcast regular programmes in the form of a schedule or timetable.

Before we can discuss how to make radio programmes we need to establish what exactly a radio programme is. There are a few different types or genres. The nature or definition will depend on whether it is broadcast live or is pre-recorded, is it daily or weekly, is it half an hour or three hours, will it be repeated, how is it structured and what does it contain, is it a syndicated or shared programme, how is it staffed, who are its audience?

Stations now broadcast 24 hours a day, but this does not mean all of their output is generated by the station teams and only broadcast once in the schedules. For most stations, though not all, daytime is when they achieve their best listening figures. The peak is at breakfast time from about 6 am–9 am and in the afternoon once school ends and when people are travelling home from their workplaces – known as drivetime. So these are the times when they will feature their best presenters and material. Stations in the same group, or in the BBC, region or cluster share programmes during off-peak times like overnight (midnight–6 am) or take sustaining services provided by another station. BBC Radio 4 for example, despite being a national service, carries selected BBC World Service programme material. In the past BBC local radio carried Radio 2 overnight when it was the only BBC service to run 24 hours a day, then some took 5Live when it became a 24-hour news service, now some, like Radio Newcastle, set up their computer with music and links to run automatically through the night, thereby retaining a form of local identity. Some ILR stations do the same or share or syndicate a programme across a

number of stations owned by the same group. If you can come up with the right
format, for example, for a chart show, specialist music or themed music programme
in a style that could sit comfortably across a range of stations across the country
and find a presenter that has wide audience appeal then you could be onto a winner
for syndication. Stations keep their individuality by including their idents, promos
and ads in specific time slots. Commercial stations' output relies mostly on music
and there have been calls for them to consider developing and sharing the cost
of producing some sort of high profile but occasional syndicated speech programming that would broaden their output. Commercial stations like those of the
BBC have also joined forces to raise money for charity appeals or awareness-raising
campaigns. Stations also broadcast a choice of listening to alternative programme
material on their different frequencies, for example speech and gold music selection on medium wave for the mature listener and chart music on FM for the
younger target audience. BBC Radio 4 will offer its usual programmes on its FM
frequency, but offer its listeners live coverage of a major cricket match on LW (long
wave).

Weekends will often see a change of pace, programming and presenters with less
emphasis on hard news and time checks and more entertainment and music.

Some programmes are also repeated, sometimes in a different time slot on the same
day as the original broadcast or later in the same week or at the weekend, when there
may be a different audience. This particularly applies to stations that use features,
documentaries, comedy and drama.

A live or recorded radio programme is a collection of voices, music and sounds,
sometimes containing all these elements, a combination of two or simply just one
of them. They are mixed together into different forms or modes of delivery of various
durations and put into a running order or sequence to result in a programme. Many
live programmes will have fixed time slots for some of their items: for example, in
a breakfast time programme you will hear news bulletins on the hour, headlines or
summaries on the half hour, travel at 15, 30 and 45 minutes past the hour and sport
at 20 minutes past the hour. Recorded audio material is stored on the studio
computers and played out by the presenter at the appropriate time. Written text in
the form of cues, links, news and other information that the presenter needs to read
out can also be stored and accessed, making the studio paper and tape-free.

VOICES AND WORDS

Copy

This is a story in written form read aloud by the presenter within the programme.
For example:

People signed off as long-term sick are being encouraged to head back to work. The Government's hoping its new drive will get a million people off Incapacity Benefit within ten years.

Claimants will be offered incentives to job hunt and threatened with a cut in payments if they don't.

Copy and clip

This refers to the above example but is one which would also include a short extract of illustrative audio from an interview with the Work and Pensions Secretary. The clip would be introduced by another short line of copy setting it up: 'But as Work and Pensions Secretary John Hutton explains measures need to be taken to save taxpayers billions of pounds a year.'

Voice piece, voice report or voicer

This is a live or recorded report written and read by a correspondent or reporter into a programme or news bulletin. The duration can vary from about a minute to about ten depending on station policy and the nature of the programme. For example:

Newsreader: People on long-term sickness benefit are being encouraged back to work. John Smith has the details.

John Smith: The Government is hoping that it will get a million people off Incapacity Benefits within ten years by offering a package of carrot and stick measures. The Department of Work and Pensions says that Incapacity Benefits cost the taxpayer twelve and a half billion pounds a year. Tony Blair insists that the proposed measures shouldn't be seen as a crackdown on scroungers. He says this is about helping people who find themselves virtually stranded living on the State. He still has to convince Labour backbenchers that they'll work.

Wrap

The same as a recorded voicer, but also containing a short extract of audio, maybe from an interview, at its centre: in the example above this could be from an interview with a politician. The spoken report by the correspondent or reporter is wrapped around the audio before and after the clip.

Package

Like a wrap but longer and more detailed. Again it would need to be introduced into the bulletin or programme by a cue from the newsreader or presenter. It will contain links written and read by the reporter, extracts from interview material, a vox-pop, appropriate actuality and sometimes music to add emphasis, context and texture. The package can be used to put across complex and diverse topics in an accessible, concise and imaginative way. It offers the reporter the opportunity to produce a considered piece of journalism. It can be used as a method of providing background to a story or as a method of pulling together earlier events. The success of a package relies on the interviewing skills of the reporter, their storytelling ability and some nifty editing and mixing. Many a story that is mundane or lacking in real substance has benefited from the package treatment.

How would you convert the example used above into a package?

A good package will be creatively produced. For example:

A new series of a popular children's science fiction TV programme is to be screened with a new actor playing the part of the eccentric hero. A basic package on this subject lasting about 90 seconds could be made up as follows.

• Theme music from the series. (6 seconds)

• Spoken link from the reporter. (10 seconds)

• Clip from an interview with the actor playing the title role. (18 seconds)

• Link from the reporter. (6 seconds)

• Clip from an interview with the TV critic of a national newspaper. (15 seconds)

• Link from the reporter. (6 seconds)

• Vox pop with children and parents about the series. (15 seconds)

• Link from reporter. (8 seconds)

• Theme music from the TV series (6 seconds).

Notice the link/clip/link/clip structure of the storytelling sandwiched between some appropriate music. The package could be more sophisticated in its production through the use of sound effects and perhaps sequeing some of the material to reduce the need for reporter links, longer in length and include more interview material with say actors who have played the lead role in the past or the series producer. The links are important as they guide the listener through the story and give the report structure. The clips should be the strongest sounding that you can find from the longer interview and they should add something to the story, not just illustrate what has been said in the links.

How much time would you allocate to each of the segments in the running order above? Would you prefer the music to run as a bed throughout the whole piece, perhaps peaking at certain points to add pace and colour to the speech? What other speech, music or sounds would you like to add to the basic package?

There is an ongoing debate amongst radio broadcasters about the future of the package. It centres around a number of working practice issues and the contrasting modes of delivery adopted by radio. Some editors see the package as an expensive means of telling a story. After travelling to collect interviews and then time in the production process a reporter can spend a working day producing three minutes of radio which may only receive one or two plays on air. During that time they could have spent their time on the telephone arranging a number of live interviews that would provide programme presenters with plenty of material. The reporters, however, argue that they didn't become broadcast journalists to spend all their time 'phone bashing' for interviewees for someone else to interview especially as they probably dug up the story, researched the background, found the contact and can come up with some excellent questions to put to them. Then the 'live' argument comes into play. Live radio's chief attractions are its immediacy, spontaneity and responsiveness and from a cost viewpoint live radio is cheaper to produce than recorded, which has to be a consideration when you are operating on a limited budget. As usual many agree on the compromise – that radio output should offer a mix of textures. It can also be argued that the method of storytelling should be dependent on the content of the story and that the most appropriate method should be chosen.

How do you stand on this debate? Would your viewpoint change if you were an editor or a reporter? If you were employed on a station how would you prefer to spend your working day? Which mode of delivery of a story do you think the listener prefers? Are you for crafted, considered pieces that may be seen as not cost effective? Or do you want more live responsive radio content that could be seen as simply a series of talking heads?

Feature

A mainly speech-based piece on a particular subject and similar to a package, but usually longer and in more depth. It may also use additional audio material like diary or newspaper extracts, further interviews, archive material etc. to tell a complex or multilayered story. A feature could be made up using combinations of other forms of audio delivery, for example, by using a mix of material from an interview and extracts from an audio diary featuring the same person. The feature can be a stand-alone item in its own right or be included as part of a programme. So, using the children's TV series story above as an example, the feature would probably explore a wider area by examining other issues and historical angles rather than just the focused angle of the package. A feature might explore the changing nature of the character of the hero or the series' impact on a range of different generations of viewers from the 1960s when the series started to the present young audience.

Montage

This technique can be applied to a number of storytelling forms, in particular features and documentaries. It is favoured when attempting to produce a more impressionistic effect. This is perhaps why it is regarded by some as an 'arty' way of producing radio. Material is not linked by a presenter or reporter but tells its story by juxtaposing the voices, actuality and music. Without the benefit of these links to guide the listener it is up to the producer to offer up signposts and labels for them. Careful consideration needs to be given to the structure of the whole and sequencing of the individual contributions. The longer the montage the more complicated it is to produce and the more challenging it can be for the listener. Mini-montages can also be used to act as scene-setters at the start of programmes, to illustrate a theme or concept during a programme or to summarise views at the end.

Interview

This is a question and answer segment with the programme presenter or inter-viewer asking a guest or contributor questions about a particular story. Interviews can be conducted live or be pre-recorded. Longer interviews with a main guest could be divided up into smaller segments with breaks for music tracks between the speech.

Here are a few guidelines to make sure you come back with a recording you can use if you are planning to record an interview using a portable recorder:

- Test the equipment and take along some spare batteries.

- Know where you are going, who you are interviewing and what you want to ask them.

- If the interview is to be indoors choose a suitable room: a small office with plenty of soft furnishings is preferable to a large boardroom acoustic. Even indoors extraneous and intermittent noise can ruin your recording so listen out for that ringing telephone, music, loud voices outside in the corridor and so on. Microphones can also pick up the humming sound generated by overhead fluorescent lights and from refrigerators and computers. If you are not happy with the location suggest politely that you need to move and explain why.

- Stand or sit next to your interviewee rather than directly in front of or too close to them and certainly not across a desk from them.

- If you are recording outdoors be aware that the microphone will need to be sheltered from the wind otherwise your interview will be punctuated with a distracting bumping sound.

- Listen out for those noises in the background that could be picked up on your recording like traffic, passing aircraft, lawnmowers and dogs barking.

- Check the levels of your own voice and that of your interviewee.

- Wear headphones to help check your recording as it progresses.

- During the interview try not to move the microphone and its cable around too much otherwise you will get the sound of microphone rattle on your recording.

- Hold the microphone upright or at a slight angle to the speaker just below or to the side of their mouth. Too close and you will hear what is known as popping on the recording.

- It's a recording so don't be afraid to record any parts of the interview that you are not happy with, and that includes your questions.

- Get your interviewee to introduce themselves and any other relevant information like job title on the recording so you will be able to identify the interview amongst all the others you may be doing that day and know how to pronounce their name if it is an unusual one.

- Before you leave the location check that the interview has been recorded and saved. If for example you forgot to switch on the recorder or failed to put it into record mode then admit your mistake and ask if you can try again. It's better to face this embarrassment than the wrath of your editor on your return from a wasted journey.

In the studio you are on home territory and hopefully less can go wrong with your broadcast or recording. There are of course procedures you should follow to get the best technical quality.

- Check the levels of your voices before you go to air. Watch the meters and monitor what you hear during the interview.

- Keep an eye on the clock.

- Make sure the interviewee is correctly positioned in front of the microphone and ask them to stay quietly in their seat once the interview is over until the microphone is no longer live.

- Warn them that during the interview you may have to look away sometimes to check that everything is working and to carry on speaking as though nothing is happening.

- Ask them to turn away from the microphone if they need to cough or clear their throat.

Two-way

This is an interview where the correspondent or reporter takes on the role of interviewee and answers questions from the presenter of the programme. The correspondent or reporter may be in the same studio and across the table from the presenter, linked by line from another studio or from a location at the scene of an event or incident. The overall feel of a two-way interview is different to reporting in that it will sound like an unscripted, informed conversation. The two-way can be very useful if a story has just broken and information is still sketchy, if there has been a new development and your reporter is on the scene or has access to information not yet made public, or indeed if your correspondent has specialist knowledge about the subject or topic of the story. There is a trend towards following up a pre-recorded background package made by the reporter with a follow-up live two-way for an update once it has been aired. The two-way also comes into its own when there is a running story – that is a story that continues to yield copy throughout the day such as a disaster, trial or hostage incident. The correspondent or reporter is expected to be clear-headed, have an acute news sense and be able to think on their feet. Remember too that as a story unfolds information comes from a range of sources, some of which will be picked up by the reporter on the scene and some directly into the newsroom. The two-way is not an easy option as it can fail to convince and sound contrived. Both participants should know the story and be aware of the questions that will be asked and the likely answers. This helps make sure no one sounds stupid, that there are no legal or privacy reasons for avoiding certain questions and with time limited will ensure the story gets told succinctly. Time, as usual, is a limiting factor so it is important that all concerned know how much time is being allocated to the interview: after all the reporter needs to make sure they have enough information to talk about in the slot. What time is the piece going on air? Time needs to be allowed to set up the link between the studio and the reporter on location.

The two-way is also sometimes referred to as a Q & A – question and answer.

Vox pop

This is a recorded selection of comments from members of the general public questioned in the street about a topic or issue. The reporter's voice asking the question, which is the same to all the interviewees, is usually left out of the final piece. A vox pop will often be used to act as a taster, scene-setter or stimulus for a studio discussion or phone-in. They also pop up in some packages or features. There are mixed feelings about collecting and constructing material for vox pops amongst reporters. Some love doing them and others dislike them. If you are just getting started in radio or if you are on a station for work experience or industrial placement chances are that you will be sent to do a vox pop and the result is often used as a measure of your abilities by your editor. Don't think that if you make a bad job of it then you will not be asked again – chances are you will be sent out until you get it right. Here are some tips to help achieve good results:

- Make sure you know what the vox pop is supposed to be about. What is the topic? Check that the editor is happy with the question you intend to ask your interviewees: it should be an open question that allows them to offer up more than simple one word answers.

- Find out how long the finished product has to be. There are no set rules about how many people you need to interview to fill your time slot – it will depend on how long they speak for and how much you decide to edit. Record as many as you like and stop when you think you have enough useful material.

- Check your recording equipment is working properly before you leave the station.

- Choose your location carefully: you want your piece to have some atmosphere and texture but avoid over-noisy places or where intermittent noise is likely. Background noise will make editing your clips that bit more difficult. A shopping precinct or marketplace where the noise provides a constant background atmosphere should generally be fine and of course there should be plenty of people about to talk to.

- You will always find people in a bus queue and because they have nothing to do but wait for the bus and as they won't usually be going anywhere until it arrives hopefully they will be glad to talk to you. Another consideration should be appropriateness – if you are collecting reactions to the news that the town's swimming pool is to close down then you know which location you should be heading for.

The most nerve-racking part of the process for the inexperienced vox popper is making those initial approaches to members of the public in the street. Accept the fact that you will be rebuffed. Try to wear a badge with the station logo on it or one that clips onto the microphone. Holding the microphone by your side make your initial approach towards your potential speaker. You should keep your opening comments short – 'Hello, local radio news can I ask you about how you keep warm in winter?' – bringing the microphone up between you.

The person may ignore you and walk on, in which case you leave them be. They may keep on walking but give you a reply in which case you trot after them saying, 'Hang on, say that again for me once I've switched on the microphone' and record them and possibly ask a supplementary question based on their reply.

Try to collect answers from a wide range of voices offering a number of views or opinions and it is imperative that the technical quality of your location recordings is high.

As a safeguard, before you leave the location record a minute or so of the general background atmosphere that you may want to run underneath the interviews to hide any untidy edits.

Back at the station download the answers you want to use into the computer, don't waste time with those you know that you don't want, and try them out in different orders and juxtapositions until you have the permutation that sounds best.

Here are some possible replies to the question about keeping warm from a range of age groups. Structure them into a running order for a vox pop then write a cue sheet to introduce the piece.

- 'Funny you should ask that, I'm just off to buy a new overcoat' (Female 50s)

- 'Oh, I never feel the cold' (Male 30s)

- 'Turn up the central heating and snuggle up to the wife' (Male 50s)

- 'Snuggle up to my boyfriend' (Female 20s)

- 'How do I keep warm? A drop of brandy in my morning coffee' (Male 60s)

- 'I hate the cold. I always wear lots of layers of clothes and stay indoors in front of the fire' (Female 40s)

Phone-in

This can be either a segment within a programme or a programme in its own right (see Chapter 5). Listeners to the programme are encouraged to phone in on a special number that will link them to the studio team who are able to put them on air and talk with the presenter and their studio guests. Some programmes invite calls but don't put the callers on air; comments are passed to the presenter who will read them out. Listeners are also invited to write letters and email their comments to the studio and these too will be read out by the presenter. It is important that if the invitation is offered the programme provides a forum in which it can respond or at least feature this interactivity.

Discussion

When more than one guest interviewee is taking part in a programme either in the live studio, down the line or on the telephone at the same time rather than separately it is referred to as a discussion or debate, sometimes known as a 'round table'. A short discussion can be included as part of a programme or, as described in Chapter 5, can be the actual programme. Unlike general interviews the guests are expected to pick up from each other's comments and interact rather than wait for the next question from the presenter. However, it is up the presenter to make sure everyone gets a fair opportunity to speak up and put their point of view.

Audio diary

This method of reportage can be compulsive listening. It involves a reporter or contributor recording their personal involvement in a story together with their thoughts and feelings at the time. Using a portable recorder they speak directly to the listener. The best ones will also record actuality of their activity to add atmosphere and colour to the piece. It's a bit like a voice report but unscripted and informal and can be used as a stand-alone item or as part of a programme. The results can be full of insight, tension and humour but they do lack intervention of a reporter who could challenge and question the contributor. A good producer, however, should be able to edit and mix the material in conjunction with input from the contributor and create a useful piece of radio.

It is important that the contributor, if they are not a professional broadcaster, is given training in the technical operation of the recorder and microphone to ensure the best quality of sound recording. This method can be useful for getting recordings from usually inaccessible places. A few years ago it was announced that a light tower in the English Channel was to go automatic which meant that the team of light tower keepers who worked the manning rota and had to be flown out by helicopter would no longer be needed. Because no one other than the keepers were allowed on the huge tower, the radio station I was working for decided it would be a good idea to give one of the men a portable recorder so that he could record the final week of the tower being operated by a human being. Unfortunately the diary was never used as the keeper thought the recorder was on when it was in fact off and vice versa, so nothing that was recorded was broadcastable.

I have heard interesting audio diaries recorded by a listener giving birth for the first time, a listener who was walking up Mount Kilimanjaro for charity and a day in the life of a road sweeper. Audio diaries make regular appearances on podcasts too.

Making an audio diary can be a useful exercise for those new to audio production as it can help develop a number of the skills and techniques required for more advanced radio production and can be as simple or as complex as you want it to be. You might like to keep an audio diary following your attempt to give up smoking or eating chocolate. In your first entry you could explain what you are doing, what you hope to achieve and why. It could include the actuality of you smoking your hopefully final cigarette or munching your favourite bar. The second entry could be about how you are feeling and coping. Later entries will probably be about how you did or didn't resist temptation and the physical and psychological effects the withdrawal signs are having on you.

Set yourself a time limit for the recording period and the final piece otherwise there will be so much material that you will become bored while editing it down to a reasonable length. Make sure the piece has an interesting ending.

This exercise will give you an understanding of the audio diary techniques that you will be able to pass on to a future contributor, experience in speaking spontaneously on microphone, developing microphone techniques, telling a story, editing and mixing.

Oral history

Collecting the memories of people by recording their voices either for use in a radio programme or for an audio archive is a very satisfying exercise. The events they describe may be personal or have wider implications but in both cases we hear reminiscences that are first-hand experiences. BBC projects like *The Century Speaks*, *20th Century Vox* and *My Century* have made good use of this kind of material in programme making and in providing archive material. The techniques used for collecting such material and making programmes from it demand a slightly different approach to production. Collecting the material should be more time-consuming than regular interviews. The contributor should be relaxed and unhurried, allowing them to describe events at their own pace uninterrupted by questions. In order to avoid the sometimes intimidating presence of a microphone clip-on lapel mics can be used. The interviewing duration will be longer and therefore more tiring (and sometimes emotionally draining) so be prepared to take breaks and take time to relax with the contributor after the recording.

When each of the items listed above is featured in a programme it will need to be introduced by the presenter in the form of a cue that explains to the listener what they are about to hear.

MUSIC

This will be chosen before the programme goes on air and will be available for the presenter to play in various forms. Recorded music will be on compact disc (CD), minidisk (MD), vinyl records or tape. Music tracks are also stored on computers in the studio and the presenter will be able to drop them down from the library into a programme playlist and then play them by clicking a mouse or touching the screen which lists the tracks. The computer playout system will also show information about the music. As well as the title, name of the performer and duration and pace of the piece, useful details such as length of the opening instrumental introduction before the vocal begins and whether the track fades or ends is given.

Most commercial recording agreements with stations allow almost unconditional use of music on the radio. Musicians and record companies welcome exposure on air to help promote sales.

Music is often used in packages, trails and advertisement production and copyright clearance needs to be arranged and paid for. To help keep down costs it is possible to access 'library music' which is free of copyright restrictions, but must still be entered on the music reporting logs and is much cheaper. This is made up of collections of musical themes and atmospheres on CDs that have been specially produced by music production companies. The CDs will contain several different duration versions of each of the tracks – say 15, 30, 45 and 60 seconds – which the producer can select as a bed for their trail or ad.

Music of course is also performed live in programmes. MCPS costs are not applicable because it is not a commercial recording. Composers and publishers rights will be covered by PRS blanket agreement and Musicians Union (MU) fees will need to be paid to the performers.

The BBC also has a collection of music referred to as 'non-needletime'. They acquired broadcasting right free from PPL payments. The material is often remixed versions from original studio recordings and published under the label 'Radioplay' for use in BBC music programmes. Their use helps reduce the number of commercial recordings in a programme, thereby lowering the cost. So instead of playing a commercial recording of, for example, 'Easy' by The Commodores the presenter could use the version available on Radioplay and save on the programmes needletime budget.

SOUNDS

Sounds in programmes add the texture and colour that can enhance the speech content. Known as FX they come in two forms, either from commercially recorded sources or actuality on location using a portable recorder and microphone.

Great care should be exercised when using sounds in your production. Listeners with sharp ears will soon berate you if you are heard to use the wrong birdsong, car engine or steam train effect.

Whenever you go on a location recording you should take some time to record a minute or so of the background sounds. These sounds are useful for scene-setting in an interview, disguising the edits in a vox pop or rounding off a package or feature.

Sounds can be used to signify a place or time – waves on a shingle beach, an owl hooting, a foghorn – without having to use words, and the passing of time or change of location can be indicated by fading out one sound, pausing and then fading in another sound.

It is also worth considering using the natural sounds or acoustic of a space as you move from say one room to another, upstairs to downstairs or indoors to outside. Another useful effect is to record the sounds of an appropriate activity conducted by a person as you interview them.

Programmes also contain and make use of other mixed content.

NEWS BULLETINS

These are often at the top of the hour every hour during the broadcast day. Some stations prefer to have their news bulletins on the half-hour or even every twenty minutes at the top of the hour, twenty past and twenty to the hour (known as 20/20 news).

Bulletins will be prepared and read by journalists working on station from a range of sources available to them. International and national news material in the form of text for copy and locally voiced voice pieces and audio for clips and wraps will be provided from GNS or IRN and from news agencies like Reuters and the Press Association (PA).

IRN for example offers those stations that subscribe to its Netnewsroom service audio clips for use in bulletins, prepared packages, latest headlines in text form for reading on air, daily prospects of stories that they hope to be covering, links to find out more about stories and links to UK police forces and councils.

This is a useful resource, according to Alec Blackman a former ILR news editor who now works in BBC LR:

> *Collecting news in commercial radio is no different to what happens at the BBC – with the exception of the resources available to you. The BBC has more reporters dedicated to just getting in stories but commercial radio may only have one of their reporters available to cover stories in a day. It makes you more reliant on press releases, phone calls and the unique contacts you have cultivated yourself at the emergency services, hospitals, council departments, courts, football clubs. You should also be on friendly terms with a schoolteacher, estate agent, bus and taxi driver as sources of information and potential stories. The average reporter spends more time in the office than on the road these days.*

Material will be researched and collected locally from emergency services (police, ambulance, fire and coastguard) from local contacts in business and industry, unions, health authorities, courts, councils etc. with audio material recorded via the telephone in the studio or newsroom or on location with a portable recorder. Once they have reported a national or international story local stations occasionally may also be looking to approach it from a local perspective for their listeners. They will also be providing their local knowledge and sending material on local stories of interest to a wider audience to their news distributing service (GNS or IRN) who will make them available to the other stations they serve.

Stations will have reciprocal agreements with their local TV stations to use material from each others bulletins, usually for an attribution mention if audio is used, for example 'The MP was asked on West TV's *West at Six* if she thought. . . .' or 'Speaking to West FM the MP explained her views . . '.

News bulletins usually last two or three minutes but it can range from one to five minutes depending on the station policy and time of day. There is more emphasis on news output during the peak listening times.

Most bulletins are known as 'mixed', which means they contain a mixture of national and local news within the bulletin. Some stations will divide up their bulletins with national and international news on the hour and local news on the half with headlines or brief summaries on the quarters.

Bulletins are like condensed programmes using combinations of copy, clip, voicer, two-way and wrap. Each news editor will have their own preferences as to how a bulletin should be written, constructed and read. Often they produce a newsroom style guide for their journalists to follow. Some prefer a bulletin that contains more copy and less audio material, arguing that more stories can be covered by copy and that audio takes up too much time in a bulletin. There is a preference for audio to be included only in bulletins longer than one minute and that it should be distributed across the start and end of the bulletin rather than only at the front. Some will only allow telephone interview clips to be included if they are about a breaking story and prefer two-ways to voicers and wraps. With such a short time slot allocated for a bulletin durations must also be strictly adhered to. Generally a bulletin lasting one minute would use four or five copy stories, a two-minute bulletin five stories with a clip or voicer and three minutes six stories plus two pieces of audio. With five stories in a two-minute bulletin a cut or clip should not exceed ten seconds, a voicer twenty seconds and a two-way 30 seconds. Although successive bulletins may contain the same stories they are 'refreshed' for each broadcast which means they are preferably updated but at least rewritten or sometimes the running order changed. If you listen to a series of bulletins through the day from one station you will notice that stories are dropped only to reappear in a later bulletin. In some newsrooms journalists will write two versions of the same story so that they can be alternated. The major rewrites of stories and the news agenda itself usually changes at lunchtime and again at drivetime.

Reading the news on air can be particularly challenging. There is a feeling that because it is serious stuff as a presenter you are under extra pressure to get it right. A bulletin will contain stories about life-changing events that will make people sit up and listen, and it is easy sometimes to forget that these events touch real people; the stories are not just something to read out in front of a microphone. After all you can't ad lib or play a jingle if things go wrong. Your approach, choice of language and presentation style needs to reflect that you are taking the job of telling people the news seriously and with authority.

SPORT

There are stations that dedicate their output to sport and others feature programmes on the subject, but some restrict themselves just to a mention in bulletins. If sports news is to appeal to a general audience who perhaps have only a passing interest in the big or local stories then the writing and presentation style needs to be closely stipulated. For example insisting on facts told in a straightforward and clear way which means avoiding clichés, jargon and over-colourful expressions but at the same time telling the stories in an entertaining way.

Coverage of a sporting event could range from a full-blown OB from the stadium with live commentary to occasional updates from a one-day game into a strip programme from a reporter watching at the ground or a single voice report into a bulletin once the event is over. Sports news bulletins often take on the same format and structure as a news bulletin.

On many local stations Saturday afternoon will include extensive coverage of their teams in action with a studio-based presenter and links to reporters at the events contributing throughout. The day usually ends with a full round-up of score-lines, league positions, reports from the correspondents, interviews with sportsmen and management. Stations build in provision for coverage of midweek events and will also try to extend coverage by having a preview programme on Friday evening and a sports round-up some time on Sunday morning reviewing the previous day's action and any fallout.

Depending on their depth and breadth of sports coverage some local stations sports teams reports are supplemented by listeners who phone in with score-lines from local matches.

JINGLES

These are used to establish and unify the station and programme identity on air. Many stations include idents known as sweepers that include the names of places around the patch where their listeners live and work and where the station can be received: 'In Midchurch, Larchester and Seeburn you're listening to Coastal Radio.'

They can feature sung lyrics, instrumental and spoken material. A radio station will commission what is known as a jingle package from a production company which contains the complete range of jingles with a unifying theme that can be used by the whole station in its programming. The news jingle for example may have two versions; one to be played before the start of the bulletin (the 'in'), drawing the listeners attention to what is to come and the 'out' when the bulletin is over. There will be jingles to head up sport, travel and weather. You will hear transitional jingles to help change the mood from a serious item into a lighter mood or vice versa or from a slow piece of music into an upbeat mood. There are production companies that can be commissioned by stations to produce a customised jingle package that can be used by them on air. Jingles come in various forms – you will come across 'beds' (music that can be played under the presenter as they speak) 'stings' and 'stabs' (that are used as a kind of punctuation between music tracks or speech items), 'idents' (that include a vocal or signature tune that identifies the station or programme), 'donut' (this contains a combination of sting at the beginning and end, with a bed at the centre) and other terms depending on which station is using them. Jingle packages also contain seasonal variations of the everyday jingles to be used at specific times of the year like Christmas or other special occasions.

Jingles can be used as signposts for the listener, notifying them about items about to be broadcast. An effective and easily identifiable travel jingle, for example, should be able to stand alone and shouldn't need re-enforcement from a presenter saying 'It's time now for the travel' before or after it has been played. The jingle should be the announcement.

ADVERTS/COMMERCIALS

Commercial radio stations have fixed time slots during their output when they feature paid-for adverts. Advertisements must be separate from the programmes, so there needs to be a definite signal to the listener that what they are about to hear is an advertisement. An ILR station would carry ads for nationally known products and local services allocating about eight minutes of airtime during peak listening times (Monday–Friday between 06.00 to 10.00) and about nine minutes at all other times. The rates that they charge advertisers just for the broadcast will vary and are available from the sales department of the station. The rates depend on the time of day and frequency of transmission.

The top rates will be charged Monday–Friday 06.00–12.00 and 07.00–13.00 at weekends. A lower rate will apply in the afternoon Monday–Friday 12.00–19.00 and 13.00–19.00 at weekends. An evening rate covers 19.00–24.00 and a night rate 24.00–06.00 all week.

The levels vary due to the limited availability of commercial airtime. The more demand, the less airtime available, thereby increasing the rate. Each commercial is usually of 30 second duration, but lengths can be varied for a fee.

Stations will usually offer a commercial production service to help clients produce a creative and effective campaign by providing the script and recording the voices, music and sounds that make up the actual commercial.

The adverts could be simply a solo voice reading a script over a music bed through to specially composed songs and music. They can use facts, humour and catchphrases to ensure that the product or service sticks in the mind of the listener. Whatever their content the best ads are usually the ones that have a single simple message sold in a creative way in a matter of seconds.

Clients will use the ads to raise awareness of a new product or service they want the listeners to sample or, if they are well established, to continue to use their products or services in preference to their competitors. It can be a real challenge to write, perform and produce ads that grab the attention and sell something in the space of a few seconds and as much planning and organising can be required for a campaign as you would spend on making a programme. In order to maintain a consistent effect for their product advertising clients will sometimes use the soundtrack from their TV ad campaign as their radio commercials, but many will argue that this doesn't always play to radio's strengths. It has also been noticed that radio listeners don't usually 'station-hop' during the ad breaks as they do when they are TV viewers.

A station will have set time slots built into its schedule for the playing of the ads. You fail to play the ad, play an ad in the wrong slot or mis-time the slot at your peril.

Presenters should never make comments of any kind about the adverts they have played.

As a listener you love them and hate them for their content or the frequency they are featured in a station's output, but they are an essential part of the station's income and pay for the news and programmes so a good sales team is a must. The quality of the ads will also reflect on the reputation of the station. Producing ads is just as simple or as complicated as making a radio package, after all they make use of the same ingredients of voices, sounds and music, and many of the production skills and values are the same. For example you need to be aware of the audience and target the style and message of the advert at them, the script needs to be prepared with as much care as news copy and above all it needs to stick in the mind of the listener. Humorous adverts will have plenty of initial impact but lack longevity qualities for sustained campaigns. The best adverts are usually simple in their message, entertaining in their storytelling and sound just that little bit imaginative. You can hear a huge range of radio ads in an archive kept by the Radio Advertising Bureau and accessed via their web site.

Any radio station licensed by Ofcom in the UK that carries advertising is governed by rules laid out in the Broadcast Committee of Advertising Practice (BCAP) Radio Advertising Standards Code. The Code aims to make sure that all the advertisements are legal, decent, honest and truthful. Ads should also be designed not to mislead or cause harm or offence. Complaints about apparent breaches of the Code are considered by the Advertising Standards Authority (ASA). Some adverts may require clearance by the Radio Advertising Clearance Centre (RACC) if they fall into special categories like advertising aimed specifically at children, medicinal products, alcoholic drinks etc. The RACC also offers advice in the writing of advertising copy in their *Radio Copy Guidelines*.

Have a go at writing some advertising copy for a service or product to be featured on a radio station of your choice. The advert will last twenty seconds. You need to prepare a script but first decide how many voices, who should voice it, will you include music or sound effects? What other information should you be asking the client to provide?

TRAILS/PROMOS

Many stations schedule programme trails or promotions into their 'clocks' so the onus is on the individual programme teams to provide a trail or promo for their programme in exchange for a number that they can feature in their programme. Some networks limit the time allocated to trails and programmes need to work hard to get trails included in the output.

Making a trail for a programme is like producing a commercial for your programme and getting it played on the programmes broadcast by your station. The difference, as Starkey (2004: 159) points out, is that unlike the advert the station bears the cost of the time and effort it takes to produce it.

Here is an opportunity to be creative and earn yourself some brownie points. Everyone enjoys and welcomes a well-made programme trail that they can include in their own programme. This shouldn't be an afterthought but be included in the production schedule. The trail will have to include specific information like the title, date and times, but the way it is produced leaves plenty of room for imaginative radio. A trail can be a pre-recorded audio package, a live voicer into a programme or a written piece of copy to be read by the other station presenters during their programmes. The trail may be a general one drawing the listener's attention to the programme, it could be looking forward to today's or tomorrow's regular edition or plugging a special edition.

Like any other audio production you should consider which voice or voices you want to use and is there room for music and/or sounds in the time you have allocated to its duration. If the programme you are trailing is already made then you might like to consider using a clip or clips from the final production.

If it is a written trail think about who is likely to be reading it on air and try and write it to suit their style. Think also about preparing and submitting two versions – one for an unspecified period leading up to the day of the broadcast and one to be read on the day prior to transmission. There is an example of a written trail in Chapter 6.

WEATHER

You could check what the weather is doing now by simply looking out of the window, but if you want a forecast of how it may change during the next day or two a service is provided by the Meteorological Office. Some stations simply use a one-sentence summary as a closing line of a news bulletin; others offer a fuller service for their listeners. Stations with a stretch of coast will want to provide information relevant to the fishing or sailing community: stations with areas of farmland or market gardening will want to provide a specialist service.

Weather reports shouldn't just help listeners decide if they should take an umbrella out with them today but offer warnings about the pollen count for hay fever sufferers and sun intensity for those who risk skin damage from over-exposure. It should never be assumed that everyone welcomes long spells of dry hot weather, even during holiday periods. There can be a tendency to present sunny weather as good news and wet weather as bad – using language like 'the weather looks good' or 'more wet weather is on the way I'm afraid'.

TRAVEL INFORMATION

Featured on national and local stations, travel news is an important part of the information service for listeners who may be in the process of travelling or planning to make a journey and will tune in to find out how they maybe affected by any problems or reassured by confirmation that all is well.

Generally the emphasis is on updates about road travel conditions and delays, but you will also find stations providing information about rail services, flights, ferry sailings and sometimes bus services.

The main bulletins are featured in regular slots particularly during the peak travel times during breakfast and drivetime shows.

Local stations will obviously focus on their immediate patch and national stations have a bit of a problem in that they can only offer a generalised picture or focus on major delays that could have a knock-on effect for a greater number of their listeners. Stations also encourage their listeners to call in with details about delays that they are experiencing, but discourage them from doing this while they are driving.

Travel information, like the weather or sport, can sometimes become news in the event of a major accident, industrial action or exceptional weather conditions.

A good travel bulletin will feature the most up to date incidents first, followed by the ongoing problems and finally, if there is time, the long-standing situations that regular listeners will probably already be well used to hearing about. The information needs to be presented with pace, but not rushed, and clear so that it is easily understood. When deciding the priority list consider which incidents will affect the greatest number of your listeners.

WHAT'S ON ANNOUNCEMENTS

The source of this material is from press releases, advertising and information provided by listeners. Many stations have forms available from the station or on their web site for organisers of local events to fill out. These are more efficient than just letters or emails because they can stipulate the information the station needs them to provide and organisers are less likely to leave out an important bit of information like the date or venue. This is a useful service that the station can provide free of charge which adds to its public service image and the sound of the localness or community involvement in its output. The information is also useful to the station as it can give them ideas and opportunities for coverage of the event as an outside broadcast, a visit from a reporter or even a chance to send along a promotional team to market the station as part of the entertainment.

COMPETITIONS

Competitions involving interactivity with the listener have always been popular whether they are just for fun or for prizes. They also give the presenter an opportunity for some light-hearted chat with a listener or two. Prizes can range from a token choice from the station's promotional material like a coffee mug to a holiday abroad. Listeners can be asked to participate in a number of activities from identifying a mystery voice, answering general knowledge questions or being the first to turn up at the station with a particular item or dressed as a chicken. Both the BBC and Ofcom have guidelines about how stations can stage competitions to ensure they are fair, appropriate and the rules made clear to participants. The BBC are not allowed to offer cash prizes and would normally pay for their prizes so tend to go for the 'original rather than expensive' but they are allowed to offer modest donated prizes like tickets, CDs and books.

IN THE STUDIO

Programmes come from a studio at the radio station. So what would you see and hear if you walked into a radio studio during the course of a programme?

The typical layout of a local station includes a production office area where the news team, programme producers and presenters work on the preparation of the broadcast. The studio area used by the production staff during a broadcast or recording is flanked on either side by the broadcast cubicles or studios. The studio will have a computer with the programme running order listed, a telephone and line answering and transfer facilities, a visual talkback computer with keyboard, a clock and a couple of loudspeakers to monitor the output of the studio and the line connections. The cubicles contain the mixing desk, microphones and playout systems on computers, CD players and MD players, computer with programme running order and email software plus the other end of the visual talkback system. Only one cubicle will be on air at a time and the other used for production preparation like pre-recording interviews, mixing features etc. The mixing desks are self-op, which means they are laid out in such a way that the presenter of the programme can operate the controls themselves without assistance; this is known as 'driving the desk'. However, the layout is such that it can be reconfigured so that the studio area can be made 'live', i.e. contain microphones for broadcast and be operated from the cubicle. This allows for more variety of programmes to be staged, for example during elections.

There is also a separate news booth where the newsreader will broadcast the bulletins into the programme. Commercial stations may also have production cubicles where advertisements for broadcast are mixed and produced.

If you see a red light come on it means that a microphone is live and being used for broadcasting or recording so you need to stay quiet unless it is you doing the broadcast.

The presenter will be sitting or standing in the broadcast cubicle, the programme producer will be in the studio area.

MIXING AND SELF-OP

Presenters on local radio will be expected to self-operate the broadcast studio for their own programme. On some BBC network stations there is some self-op and also programmes that are driven by an operator. Being driven on air means that the presenter can concentrate on their specialist role but many who self-op prefer the self-reliance, flexibility and control over the proceedings that it gives them. The biggest piece of equipment you will see is the mixing desk which can be used for broadcasting programme live or recording. You need to make sure you are in the correct mode otherwise no one will hear you or they will be able to hear when you would rather they didn't. The latest models allow an individual presenter or operator to customise and set the panel to their own requirements by choosing which fader will operate which piece of equipment. So if you prefer the far right fader to be the one that operates your microphone this can be preset and each time you work at the desk you simply load in your personal presets programme. Facing the mixing desk or panel for the first time can seem like you are being faced with the cockpit controls of an aircraft. There is a huge array of buttons, switches and faders. You are afraid to touch anything in case you accidentally take the station off air or even worse put yourself on. My first job on professional radio was as what was then known as a

PA (production assistant) where I was expected to operate the desk for a presenter, so I was given training. This knowledge put me in good stead for my future career. Once you have been shown and are more or less confident that you know what to do the secret is to practice. So if you are anticipating that you will be expected to operate a desk here are a few thoughts to get you started.

First you need to be aware that the mixing desk is there to enable you control and put the various sound sources like microphones, phones and CD players on air and if necessary put a number of combinations of those sound sources on air together at the same time. For example the presenter at their microphone and a telephone caller will both need to be on air at the same time during their conversation and a presenter may want to speak over the top of the start of a piece of music as they introduce it. On another occasion the DJ may want to fade in a CD track as another is just ending. This is called mixing. To do this entails the operation of the faders to bring the sound in, reduce its level or fade it out. Looking at a mixing desk you will see a line of faders: each one does exactly the same thing as the one next to it but for a different sound source. Each fader will be labelled with details of the sound source it is linked to. For example from left to right there may be faders for three microphones (one being for the presenter and the other two for guests or newsreaders etc.). Next in the line are the CD faders. Next may be the computer in which all the jingles and advertisements are stored and so on across the panel. Now the desk doesn't look quite so intimidating – it is simply one channel repeated. The desk will also have two faders, referred to as the main faders, which need to be open if you want the other faders to be heard on air.

To recap: in radio we talk about opening and closing faders, fading in or fading up, fading out or fading down. There are also words used to describe the different type of fade effects you can achieve. The most common is to 'dip' the sound level of a piece of music so that the DJ can talk over it as it plays in the background. Also commonly used is the 'cross-fade' when the operator fades out one source and at the same time fades in another, giving the listener an overlapping effect of the two pieces.

Under normal circumstances if you are presenting you will not fade yourself in but open the fader fully before you speak and then close it sharply the minute you have finished. It is quite common particularly, but not exclusively, amongst new presenters to forget to close the mic and bits of speech not intended for broadcast to be transmitted. If this occurs other members of the team will rush to tell the presenter via talkback to their headphones or by wild gesturing and drawing their finger across their throat to indicate that the presenter should cut their mic. Two things automatically happen in the studio when the microphone is open – a large red light switches on in the studio and another outside the studio door and the speakers that would normally be heard in the studio cut out. The lights come on as a warning to everyone that the microphone is live and the speakers cut out to avoid feedback or howl-round. Presenters need to wear headphones so that they can continue to monitor the output when the microphone is live and the speakers are off.

Just to confuse things be aware that, depending on the make of the mixing desk, the faders will be configured differently. On some models, particularly on BBC stations, you pull the fader towards you or down to open it and push it away or up to close it and on other desks it is the opposite action.

Before you put any sound on air using a fader you need to check that the levels are going to be right: not too loud and not too quiet. This need to balance the sound levels applies throughout the whole programme. If you look at one of the channels on the mixing desk somewhere near the fader you see a switch or button and an adjustable knob labelled PFL or Pre-Fade or Gain. With the fader closed and the pre-fade mode switched on you can speak into the microphone or play a CD and adjust the volume. To help achieve consistent sound levels the adjustment needs to be made in conjunction with the level meters which give a visual representation of the volume. Professional mixing desks have peak programme meters (PPM) and you should have the loudest part of a musical track (not necessarily at the start) set to be peaking between 4 and 5 and speech between 5 and 6. When you open the fader fully the reading on the meter will be the same as when it was played on PFL. It is important to remember to switch off the PFL mode once you have set levels otherwise you will not be back in position to hear the output of the whole desk. Once the levels have been set there shouldn't be any need to make any adjustments when the source is on air, but you can make minor changes by simply gently moving the position of the appropriate fader. Pre-fading of a voice or CD is carried out while another CD or recording is being played to air and the microphone is closed.

MONITORING

There are three ways to monitor the output of the mixing desk: by listening via your headphones or the studio speakers and by watching the needle moving on the meters. They should be used in conjunction. The volume according to the meters is the true volume as far as the listener is concerned as the headphone and speaker volumes are personal preferences of the presenter or technical operator and used alone would give a false impression. Monitoring selectors operated from the desk will offer a number of alternatives. For example the same selector could be set to monitor the output of the station as it will be heard by the listener, the output of the studio you are sitting in or of another studio elsewhere on the station or from a remote studio. If you are on air you should be monitoring the output as it leaves the transmitter, not via the facility that allows you to monitor the signal being sent from the studio to the transmitter. This is the only way you will know for sure that you have gone off air. Do not assume, however, that all the transmitters that broadcast your station's programmes have failed. If you think you have gone off air carry on as usual and monitor the studio output only while you get the engineers to find out what has happened.

Headphones or cans are a very important part of the presenter's studio equipment. Not only are they useful for monitoring station or studio output but also for communication purposes. The headphones can be split by operating a switch on the mixing desk – usually next to the headphone volume control – so that the presenter can listen to the programme in one ear and messages via talkback from someone in the next door studio, a remote studio, the radio car or a telephone caller. Using headphones in conjunction with the pre-fade and talkback facilities a presenter can confirm the presence of a contributor, speak to them off air and check their levels. Producers and other studio staff will try not to use talkback to a presenter's headphones when they are speaking on air as this can be distracting; however, practised broadcasters don't seem to mind and can keep talking and acknowledge the message without a hint of a pause. If a producer for example has to use audio talkback then they usually speak softly and keep the message brief or use the visual talkback system for longer messages or instructions.

If you are recording a programme in the studio, either as it is broadcast live for perhaps a repeat slot or a programme for later transmission, you should also monitor the recording as it progresses. So if the recording is on to a MD every now and then switch to the PFL of the MD recorder channel to check everything is being copied then switch back to monitoring the broadcast.

4
Making programmes

How is a radio programme made? Who does what and when? In this chapter we go behind the scenes and consider the basics of preparation and organisation before, during and post-production.

In their books about radio Paul Donovan (1997), Sue MacGregor (2002) and Libby Purves (2002) give valuable insights into the production of BBC Radio 4's long running flagship breakfast news magazine programme *Today* and the two women, along with Olive Shapley (1996) in her autobiography, describe the pleasures and pitfalls of working on *Woman's Hour*, another topical magazine programme on the same network.

Because of the demands for programmes to fit into a station's structure and the pressures on broadcasters to fill their slots, meet deadlines and stay in budget it follows that, as Hendy (2000: 70) points out, producers and their team develop routines and systems around the production to help them cope and that this naturally impacts on the sound and content of the programme. A long-running weekly music programme that I, and many other producers, worked on for BBC Radio 2, involved recording the same musicians and singers in the same studio season after season. The mood and style of the programme demanded that the mixing desks levels, tone controls and faders, along with the positioning of the microphones were set according to a laid-down master plan for each recording. The overall effect created a familiarity of style of arrangement and content that the listener came to expect every time they tuned in.

In most cases each programme you work on may well sound and contain something different, but like any other job there are tasks, some dull, that accompany the creativity required by the programme maker and there can be those 'head in hands' moments of despair when all the planning falls apart. Each member of the production team will develop their own methods and routines of working, especially if they are working on a regular programme. However, this should not stop them from being excited, creative and imaginative about the way they need to work. It is easy so slip into those short-cut routines for the sake of time saving, simplicity and an easy life that can lead to predictable and similar sounding radio.

There is a saying among broadcasters – 'You are only as good as your last programme'. As far as live broadcasts are concerned, no matter how well you have prepared the programme you should always expect the unexpected. Sometimes things do go wrong on air and you will be judged by how you coped with the crisis. If the listener is unaware of things going awry then you have done a good job.

As a programme maker you need to rehearse and hear the programme and the stages of production in your head. This can help with planning, help you to anticipate problems and assess its potential.

Let's follow a fictional programme from start to finish and examine the preparation and organisation needed from the team before and during the programme. As an example we'll choose a live weekly personality-led music and speech mix sequence programme for a national audience. As well as the microphone talent the team consists of a producer who will also studio produce the programme on air, two researchers, a production assistant and a studio manager or technical operator. The programme is broadcast for two hours on a Saturday morning and is contracted to provide two ten-minute interviews in the first hour and a main twenty-minute interview spread over the second hour. The rest of the programme is made up of music and chat including some listener requests, correspondence from listeners, at least two trails for other programmes on the station and a competition with live listener participation.

Monday

Production meeting with the team. Debrief on previous Saturday's programme. Progress on future planning for later editions of the programme – guests booked and any themed items or specials that are in the pipeline. Plans and confirmed bookings etc. for this week's programme. Presenter unable to attend this meeting due to other appearances but the previous programme will have been discussed with the producer, feedback given on performance and ideas and comments from the presenter passed on to the rest of the team. Ideas for guests, items and specials are offered up – everyone is expected to be able to come along to the meeting with a handful of ideas and participate in high-energy brainstorming sessions to develop them. Ideas come from a myriad of sources – there is the fortnightly *Broadcasters Bulletin* with details of who is touring the country, film premières, theatre first nights etc. indicating who may be available for an interview, you may have heard people talking in the pub the night before that sparked off a suggestion for a discussion, your little brother may be raving about the latest fad amongst schoolchildren or something you read in the latest edition of a specialist magazine. Programme teams often keep a diary in which they can note forthcoming events, anniversaries and ideas suggested by listeners that they can consult regularly. After the meeting researchers continue with booking guests that have been approved by the producer. Producer and researchers plough through press and publicity releases and other material (books, CDs, videos etc.) sent by agents, agencies, publishers and record companies for consideration by the team for the programme. Production assistant opens and discusses mail sent by listeners for any potential material (music requests and dedications, interesting anecdotes and questions) that could be included in the programme. Presenter will be carrying out own research by reading, listening to or watching relevant material like books, TV programmes, music and so on linked to guests due to take part in Saturday's programme and preparing questions and other scripted material they will be using.

Tuesday

Producer chooses music to be used in next programme and liaises with studio manager about any technical requirements and problems that are likely to occur for the programme. For example one guest in the first hour will not be joining the presenter in the studio but linked from a satellite studio in another part of the country. The main guest in the second hour will be playing a song or two on their guitar live during the programme.

Researchers research guests and prepare interview briefs for presenter.

Production assistant liaises with guests or their representatives about travel and other arrangements to ensure they are clear about where and when they should be on Saturday morning. The PA also organises any correspondence or follow-ups to last week's programme, for example sending out the competition prize and signed photos of the presenter to those listeners who requested them. The programme's web site is also updated with details and extracts from the last programme and promotional material about the next programme.

Wednesday

A problem has developed that needs to be sorted out immediately. The second guest due to appear in the first hour calls to say they will not be able to come to the studio for the live appearance. The production team decide that the guest can only really be included in this week's programme rather than a future one because of the topicality of the subject they are coming in to talk about. It is decided that they will try to arrange for the presenter and the guest to be at the studio earlier on Saturday before the programme or if not the day before to pre-record the interview.

Thursday

The producer draws up the running order of the programme for Saturday including the selection of music, guests and other inserts and material ensuring everything is timed and that there is enough material to fill the programme. The running order should be copied to everyone involved in the programme together with the written cues prepared by the presenter in conjunction with the producer or researcher. Experienced presenters will usually write their own cues in a style and language that suits their presentation. Good producers will leave some flexibility in the running order in case items over-run their time slot or indeed under-run. Extra music tracks should be made available in case of emergencies – like a guest not turning up. It is also a good idea to include a pre-recorded timeless item as a standby filler to cover for this eventuality. It could perhaps be a feature that was recorded with the presenter on location. Extra written material that could be used by the presenter to fill in time lasting from a few seconds to a minute is another good safeguard against minor emergencies: some written programme trails, details of guests due on the programme in the future, news about a new competition you will be introducing soon and letters and emails from listeners.

Friday

Double-check that everything is ready for the programme tomorrow. Has all the paperwork been completed and distributed? Have all the music tracks been listened to and checked for faults? Are the pre-recorded trails, jingles, station idents and adverts if applicable available in the studio playout systems?

Saturday

Arrive at the studio in good time – depending on how much needs to be set up for the programme. The studio producer and studio manager/tech op will have set up the studio and cubicle and tested that the microphones and other equipment are working.

Conduct a 'top and tail' rehearsal of the opening and closing of the programme and any other tricky sequences. If there are a lot of inserts also carry out a 'top and tail' of the cues and back announcements.

Before you go live make sure everyone has switched their off mobile telephones.

If the programme was well prepared and organised, everyone knew what was expected of them, communication between the team was clear and minimal and everyone including the listener enjoyed it then you had a good programme.

After the programme make a new general trail for the programme and provide a written trail specifically for next week's edition.

Leave the studio as you would hope to find it.

COMPLIANCE

All producers of radio programmes should take adequate precautions to ensure that the programme they broadcast will not cause offence or break the law. During live programmes the dangers are at their highest. Commercial radio stations transmit with a few seconds delay which means the broadcasters can have more control over the output should they need to block out anything that could cause problems, say during a public phone-in. BBC stations rely on screening and briefing before putting a contributor on air.

All recorded programmes submitted to the BBC for broadcast must be accompanied by a completed compliance form and submitted to their Compliance Officer. This is to ensure that guidelines relating to the interests of the listener and contributors, good practice, broadcast law, copyright and safety have been followed by the producer and potential problems can be addressed before transmission. It is also an Ofcom regulation.

The staff producer or independent production company is expected to answer yes or no to a series of questions and provide further information if they answer yes. Provision of further detail is in most cases voluntary but there are certain areas where this detail must be submitted. The list is comprehensive and applicable to any programme TV or radio produced for the Corporation. The *Editorial Guidelines* published by the BBC is a good reference point as it outlines the best practice and their procedures. They give a useful insight into why the compliance questions are being asked.

Here are the questionable areas applicable to radio productions listed more or less verbatim from the compliance form together with some of my own observations.

- Does the programme content raise any legal issues? Has a lawyer been consulted about any potential legal issues?

- Does the production contain any strong language or other language (e.g. blasphemy) that may offend? You will be required to give details and name the BBC person who authorised it. The Corporation gets more complaints from the public about language used on air than any other subject. It may be necessary to issue a warning to listeners before the broadcast and it may also mean rescheduling the broadcast to a later time slot.

- Does the programme include any sexual content – either descriptive or innuendo? Problems can arise in drama, comedy and even discussion programmes and interviews if a scene or language is too descriptive.

- Are you aware of any content which may appear to condone anti-social, illegal or dangerous behaviour? Children and young people are particularly vulnerable to this type of material and something broadcast may lead to imitative behaviour.

- Is there any potentially contentious portrayal of disabled people, religious groups or minorities?

- Consider any descriptions of violence, disasters, accidents or kidnapping, real or fictional, that could make disturbing listening. It is worth noting that complaints were received when Mark Tully as the BBC's India correspondent described and used actuality recordings of a goat being sacrificed in Pakistan.

- If the programme includes interviews with criminals, especially if they are discussing their crime, you will need to name the interviewee and the BBC person who authorised it.

- You should give details about any public figures who act as contributors or presenters or if there are any references to public figures. Issues about conflicting interests (actual or potential) and defamation may need to be raised.

- Does the programme contain any surreptitious recording? You will need to name the BBC person who authorised it as this method of collecting material is seen as a last resort. The BBC's *Editorial Guidelines*, those of Ofcom and the NUJ are very clear about the purposes and methods of secret recordings.

- On the question of impartiality, does the programme deal with matters of public or political controversy? You will be required to give details. Is there personal view or 'authored' content which is not balanced within the programme? It is worth noting here that you are not being asked to provide the balance – some programmes or contributions will be personal opinion.

- Dramatic representations of living people or people with close living relatives need to be accurate. You will be required to name them and give details of contact made or consents sought or given.

- You will be expected to give details of any commercial references in the programme and name any references to sponsors, commercial products and brands.

You are also asked to consider any other sensitive issues apart from the above or anything else in the programme which should be borne in mind ahead of transmission or possible future repeat. For example, if you are using a member of BBC staff for presentation of the programme are you sure there are no related conflicting interests?

The compliance form also asks if the station or network has agreed any warning that would be read by continuity before the programme is broadcast and asks for the proposed text of the warning. Also the producer is asked to detail any further recommendations about transmission restrictions of the programme, for example, 'not close to children's programmes', and any additional editorial content for the audience like helpline numbers or web-site addresses.

Finally the producer must state that they have listened to the completed programme and confirm that it has been made in accordance with the BBC's *Editorial Guidelines* and is compliant for the slot commissioned.

PLANNING THE PROGRAMME

Each producer will have their own ways of planning and building their programme. A popular method of planning is to use the clock format. Instead of writing every item to be included in the programme into a list with the opening item at the top and closing one at the bottom, you slot the items into a clock face starting at the 12 o'clock position.

So 12.00 to 12.02 might be a news bulletin, 12.02 to 12.03 the opening sequence and menu with the presenter, 12.03 to 12.06 a music track and so on around the clock until you are back at 12.00, having illustrated in a more visual way the content of the first hour of the programme. This technique can be used for both speech and music programmes.

You might like to try drawing a circle and using the running order in the '*news programme*' or '*magazine programme*' part of Chapter 5 draw up a clock version by dividing each item into a segment of time to fill the hour or half-hour. Alternatively listen to an actual programme with a stopwatch, make a note of the items in order along with the duration of each one and then draw up a clock for it.

In a live sequence programme items like news bulletins, travel, weather and so on will be included in the programme clock even though they are sourced from a different area. However, bear in mind that if you are asked to produce a recorded programme you need to take into account if any time is allocated for a bulletin before the programme starts or some form of continuity announcement or trail is to be included after it ends. These will require time within the hour, so an hour long or half-hour long programme due to start after a top of the hour bulletin will need to be that duration shorter.

PRODUCTION MEETINGS

The prospects meeting where all the team meet to discuss and confirm the contents of a programme or future editions needs to be run efficiently and effectively. Everyone attending should come armed with at least one good idea. It should also be staged and managed in such a way to encourage creative thought and communication. If you are offering up new programme ideas it is vital that you put them in the context of what the opposition are offering up during that particular time slot. In other words, if your listener is not listening to your programme what else is on offer to grab their attention? Brainstorming of ideas is a technique much abused, often unintentionally, particularly by the person chairing the session. The secret is to listen as well as contribute. No idea, no matter how seemingly extreme, should be dismissed out of hand. It might form the basis for the development of another idea or if it is not appropriate today then it might be tomorrow, next week or next month. Team members should be encouraged to speak out their ideas during these sessions, but at the same time be aware that ideas need to be thought out and developed in a pragmatic way. Ideas are of little use if they are totally impractical, have little relevance to the programme or audience or are economically off limits. There is also nothing wrong in adapting ideas used by other stations or programmes; just make sure you make it your own and not a simple copy.

Fran Acheson likes people to think big and not just see programme ideas in isolation, but as part of the network or station and beyond:

People also need to be inspired to come up with new ideas and be encouraged to throw stuff into the mix. I suggest to programme makers that they should listen to two radio stations they don't usually listen to and come up with ideas and approaches based on what they hear and discuss them with the programme team in the hope that something fresh will emerge.

RESEARCH

Research is the bedrock of a good programme. If you are using web sites, newspaper or magazine articles as your first port of call to glean information be aware that what is written may not be accurate, impartial or objective. Note-taking, especially when recording quotes from interviewees, for research, future reference and as a legal or working practice requirement is a skill that should not be underestimated. Accurate and efficient notes will help avoid facts being used incorrectly, over-stated or embellished for more impact.

Here are some guidelines to help you research effectively for programmes:

• Build a contacts book that is second to none containing the names and numbers and email addresses of previous and potential guests, agents and press officers, politicians etc. who you can contact for background information and invite to participate.

• Tell your colleagues who or what you are currently working on because they may have specialist knowledge or interest and be able to offer useful material or contacts.

- Don't over research. Make sure you know how your research is going to be used. Is it for a five minute interview or an hour-long feature?

- If you work on a specialist subject or music programme keep a file of interesting articles that you find and may need to refer to later.

- If you have a preliminary chat on the phone with a guest then make a note about your own impressions of them and what they have to say. This is useful when you are discussing them with the programme producer or presenter and for future reference.

Helen Galley, who runs workshops for researchers at BBC Training, says that a good research brief for the presenter who will be interviewing a guest should be clearly laid out, accurate and contain the following:

- Name of interviewee, date of interview, duration, live or recorded, location or studio.

- Introductory note – who is the guest (singer, actor, author, representative of an organisation)?

- Peg – the reason why the programme is featuring them (start of concert tour, won award for latest performance, new book published, scientific discovery).

- Details about the peg – material gleaned from publicity material, newspaper cuttings and so on including quotes attributed to the guest. Remember that not everything printed in newspapers will be accurate and there may be corrections published in later editions.

- Information about any audio material to be featured during the interview – a track from the album, a clip from a movie and extract of the book read by the author.

- A brief biography of the guest – background, history.

- Information about what others say about them – from reviews, articles and so on including any controversial angles or quotes.

- Suggested questions or question areas – about half a dozen based on the above information.

Always keep a copy of the research brief you have prepared.

WRITING FOR RADIO

Not all spoken word on the radio is improvised. Much of what you hear has been written down and is being read aloud by the presenter: sometimes you can tell, sometimes you can't. Good presentation means that you sound as though you are telling the listener rather than reading to them, so get the script right and you are on your way to a successful programme. When writing for radio you are more likely to find yourself over-writing – that is, to say by saying too much. You should leave the listener something to do with their imagination.

If you are unsure about how you should address the listener then imagine you are sitting in a bar or café with someone and they ask you what's the latest news about a particular story or event. Obviously you would speak to them using words and phrases that you and they use in everyday conversation. Do the same on the radio.

On the BBC Radio newsroom web site Alan Little offers advice on writing for radio in which he suggests the rules for good writing are first 'have something to say', the second rule is precision, the third, beware of adjectives and finally, use words that have impact.

Remember that the listener needs to understand what is being said at first hearing. They can't ask you to say it again. Unlike reading a newspaper or book they can't glance back at the previous paragraph so keep whatever you write to be read aloud simple and clear.

As well as providing words in your script you need to provide pictures, so be imaginative with your use of language on the page so that there is a chance for the voice to lift it off the page and make whatever is written come to life in the mind of the listener.

On radio we always refer to the listener, not the listeners, because we aim to speak to our audience individually. When we address them we will write and say 'we' or 'you' rather than 'everybody'.

There are a few other basics that you need to adhere to.

In radio we don't talk about 'Mr J. Smith'. Drop the title unless it's relevant like Dr. In the first instance always give the name 'John Smith' and later in the script you can refer to 'Mr Smith'.

Says is always pronounced 'sez'.

We never drop the definite article from titles of individuals or groups 'The Prime Minister Tony Blair. . . .' 'The Japanese car makers Nissan . . .'

Numbers can be confusing on radio, so if possible round them up into a less complex total – rather than '987 new homes are to be built' say 'nearly a thousand'. This is particularly important at the start of a piece. You can always give the exact figure later in the item. However, it can be seen to be very insensitive if you round up fatalities and injury figures as part of an item about a road accident. Be accurate and factual but try to communicate the information in such a way that it stays with the listener.

Try to write actively — it makes the piece sound fresher. For example: 'Police evacuated homes in the area' rather than 'homes in the area were evacuated' and 'The task force will begin their investigations tomorrow' is better than 'Investigations will be held by the task force starting tomorrow.'

Use reported speech: 'The Minister said he would look into the situation as a matter of urgency' rather than 'The Minister said "I will look into the situation as a matter of urgency."'

SCRIPT WRITING

Clear scripts are essential to communicating a story be it a news bulletin or a documentary. The idea is to use them to produce a neat and well-ordered narrative that is written clearly, logically and directly. If you don't understand what you have written or are confused by what you read then so too will the listener.

It seems obvious to say, but it can be easy to forget that you only have one chance to make an impact. Everything you read must be instantly understandable.

By far the best method to help you get it right is to first say the words aloud and then if they sound right write them down on the page. Once it is written turn over the page and tell the story to yourself in your own words then go back to your script and change it until it sounds right.

Use one side of the page only and don't carry over an unfinished sentence to the next page.

Use a font with a size and clarity that you find easy to scan. You will need to consider how the script will be read by a presenter – from the page, in which case you should use a font such as 12 point Arial, or from a screen, in which case you will probably prefer Times New Roman and consider the screen size before you choose the font size.

Double spacing will also make the words easier to read, as will starting a new paragraph for each sentence. This will also allow some space for notations and underlining by the presenter who may want to emphasise words or insert pauses.

Try to use the simple and straightforward words and phrases that you use in everyday conversation. This will not only help you sound natural and make it easier to communicate with the listener but will also help with the delivery and pace of your presentation. Concentrate on communicating with direct active speech that speaks personally to the individual: 'If you cross the river at the small stone bridge you find yourself opposite the remains of the castle.'

Use imaginative ways of giving out basic information or facts and figures. Create pictures in the mind: 'That's enough to fill Wembley Stadium' or 'It was as high as two double decker buses.'

Write as you speak – use I'll . . . He can't . . . isn't instead of I will . . . He cannot . . . is not.

Any scripted item, be it a short three-sentence piece of news copy or documentary links, should have a strong start to grab the listener's attention, interesting development and progression through to a memorable ending.

CUE WRITING

The cue is the on-air introduction to a recording or live item about to be broadcast. If you are asked to provide a cue it should be written in such a way that it will grab the attention of the listener and make them want to hear what is about to be broadcast. The cue should contain all the information the listener needs to know to help them enjoy and understand what they hear. So it makes sense to hold off writing the cue until the item it will introduce has been completed, then you won't repeat words or phrases that might be contained in the piece.

Never underestimate the importance of the cue: it can rescue a weak piece and enhance a good one. So allow plenty of time to write it, even if it is only going to introduce a short piece of music.

The cue should lead naturally into the piece and match its mood and style but without giving away too much of the story. The best cues have a structured beginning, middle and end. There is a good example in Chapter 6.

LINK WRITING

Links help tell the story by moving it on, linking interview material clips and progressing from A to B. They are useful in that they make sense of the story for the listener. Links can simply tell the listener who has just been speaking and introduce the person who is about to speak next, but they should also contain additional information to help place the inserts or argument into some sort of context. When you edit an interview you should listen through the material you have rejected for your inserts and use the information it contains by converting it into condensed written material to form your links. Written, and therefore spoken links should be easy to understand, fit the style and length of the programme and be written specifically to fit the presentation style of the presenter.

If you watch an interview or report on television the name of the contributor is displayed on the screen as they are speaking. On radio you obviously need to identify them or credit them during the piece in your links. This should always been done the first time they are heard and again if they have not been heard for some time but appear again in the piece. This is usually done at the end of the link that introduces them and before we actually hear them speak. Another method is to allow them to speak and after the first sentence give them a short introduction and then allow the interview clip to continue with the rest of their answer or argument.

If you juxtapose two interviewees by playing one straight after the other without a link you can credit them in two different ways. If you are crediting them before the interview clips then you should end your link with the name of the first person we will hear in the inserts. If you credit them in a link after the inserts have been played then you should name the last voice we heard first.

You should try to avoid stock phrases for the words you use as the introduction to a speaker: 'Next I spoke to. . . .', 'I asked. . . .', 'To find out more I spoke to . . .', 'John Smith had this to say.'

There is a temptation to end links and cues with a question: 'So does the town need another supermarket?' This can work, but is often over-used. It's best to try and rephrase your words into a statement and use the question when you think it is entirely appropriate and imaginative.

PRESENTATION

Despite what many people think some radio presenters don't like the sound of their own voice, but if they are getting work then someone must think that they are doing something right. Even someone with a good voice needs to learn, develop and practice their presentation skills, that is microphone techniques, script reading and communicating to the listener.

Catherine Bott, who presents the *The Early Music Show* on BBC Radio 3, remembers:

> You have to present several programmes before you find your radio voice, and you do know when you have found it, and then several more before you can be completely relaxed in front of the microphone. It's interesting that you don't know what you don't know when you first start presenting. One of the first things you are taught is how to respond to the cue light so that you start speaking at the right time.

Sarah Urban advises:

> Don't forget to breathe, stay calm, pace your speaking, think before you speak and remember to think and plan at least two stages ahead during the programme so you have the next item (link, interview or CD) and the next ready to go. If you have nothing else to say then you can always fall back on a 'That was . . . and this is' type-link between music tracks but you owe it to the listener to prepare and research effectively so that you have something interesting to tell them.

Some more advice on developing your presentation skills and being a good presenter.

You should warm-up your voice before going on air. I was always advised by those giving voice training at the BBC to develop a personal routine to follow. So as I was preparing in the studio – organising the scripts, sorting the CDs and so on I would do the following:

- Whistle – to exercise the lips.

- Try a tongue twister or two to get the jaw, lips and tongue moving.

- Blow raspberries to loosen up the tongue.

- Sing to lubricate the throat and open the lungs.

- Speak the vowels using the mouth in an exaggerated way to stretch facial muscles.

- Gently clear the throat and nose

This would be followed by a breathing exercise which would be repeated if there was time:

- Exhale and empty the lungs.

- Inhale, then count to five using a projected whisper.

- Inhale, then count to five in a mid-range voice.

- Inhale, then count to five in full voice.

- Finally take a couple of deep breaths to relax.

Look after your voice. Many broadcasters recommend that you should avoid smoking or smoky atmospheres, drink plenty of water and cut down on coffee. If your voice is providing your livelihood then, like a professional singer, you need to take care of your best asset.

Open your mouth and use it fully. Nobody can see you so concentrate on sounding as good as you can for the listener. Speak at the microphone and imagine you are addressing just one person.

Posture is important. Try to sit up straight at the microphone, which should be close enough to pick you up clearly but not too close to distort the sound. Try not to move back from the mic. Keep your head up even if this means holding the script off the desk or table.

Imagine the person you are addressing (the listener) is sitting a couple of metres away from you. This will help you to remember to project your voice. Radio may be an intimate medium but you must still perform at the microphone. Find that preferred conversational ground between a mumble and a declamation.

Listening to a presenter taking a breath, sometimes a noisy breath, is very off-putting for the listener. The temptation is to take a deep breath at the start and keep going until the end of the sentence or you run out of air and then take another quick sharp breath before the next. You can hear this technique used by newsreaders who tend to breathe between stories. You should aim to keep breath in your lungs throughout and find times in your presentation when you can top them up. It helps if your script is written using short sentences.

Another irritating trait can be presenters who refer to studio activities and industry jargon or terms, especially if something has gone wrong. 'Sorry about that I must have left the pre-fade switch on, let's try that track again.' Or 'Oh, dear something seems to be wrong with the talkback.' Listeners are only interested in what comes out of the radio into their ear, not in what is going on with the equipment, and they more than likely will be alienated by your use of jargon.

Inexperienced presenters speak too quickly – I know I did when I first went on air reading the news. Write some pauses into your script to slow you down. Although it may be painful to you record your efforts, listen back and learn from the performance.

Be yourself on air – use your own voice and accent and communicate with the right amount of energy. Smile if appropriate – a smile can be heard on air. Don't be tempted to simply be a poor man's version of your favourite broadcaster.

Don't be afraid to wave your arms when giving extra emphasis: stand up if you prefer it to sitting down. Studios that are designed specially to allow the presenters and newsreaders to stand up when they perform are becoming more commonplace. Once they get used to the idea many presenters end up preferring this method, saying it gives them more freedom to move and breathe. Some presenters also prefer microphones that are attached to their headphones, rather than the ones fixed to the mixing desk, again to give them more freedom of movement as they go about their on-air performance.

Stumbling over words when reading a script is caused by:

- Inadequate preparation – make sure you read aloud a script or other written material before going on air. Check pronunciation, names, figures and sense.

- Reading too quickly – your delivery should be measured and maintain a steady pace. Concentrate as you read and read further ahead than usual. Remember to breathe freely throughout.

- Alterations to the script – a messy or untidy script will confuse you and ruin your concentration. If you make changes by hand make them clearly and if you have time retype the piece.

- Distractions in the studio – people entering and leaving, spoken messages in your headphones as you are reading, technical problems and so on. Try to ignore them but make sure they don't happen next time.

If you do stumble and you are live there's not much you can do except try again. If it's for a recording you can stop and go back to the beginning of the sentence and try again. This way makes it easier to edit.

Like an aircraft pilot who needs to put in their flying hours, make sure you put in plenty of practice even when you are not actually on air. Don't develop bad habits – monitor and record yourself to check how you sound. Have you developed an irritating verbal tic like '. . . you know what I mean?' or 'Yeah, absolutely . . .'. Get others whose opinions you respect to give you honest feedback on how they think you come across on air.

If you find yourself with a dry mouth during a broadcast with no water handy then quietly and gently try chewing your tongue with your back teeth. Simply squashing the tongue this way will release saliva. If on the other hand you find that as you speak you are generating too much saliva, then suck in air through your mouth with your tongue behind your teeth and the incoming air will dry out the liquid.

If you are nervous or unsure about broadcasting at the microphone you may find that the slightest thing going wrong or a remark by a member of the team will start you laughing at a time when you shouldn't. This is known as corpsing. If you get a fit of the giggles you need to refocus as quickly as possible. Try looking away from the source of your amusement – the ceiling is usually a good place. You could also try thinking sad or serious thoughts (like 'if I don't stop giggling I will get the sack') or think about how amateurish this must look to others or as an extreme tactic dig your nails into your hand or pinch yourself so that the sudden pain distracts you. You should then be able to carry on.

Remember presenting a programme is about performance. One DJ I watched through the window of the studio was really animated. The opening link of his show over a music bed went something like this: (Holding up hand in greeting) 'Hello'. (Arms outstretched) 'Welcome to the show' (Punches the air). 'We've got some great things lined up for you today' (Counts off the list on his fingers). 'Tim Smith will be here to answer your questions about holiday destinations, there's our competition where you could win a grand and an *Eastenders* heart-throb will be talking about his new CD . . .' The presenter's enthusiasm for the programme really came across and had much more impact than if he had just been sitting down with his hands on the faders.

The first piece of music he then introduced and played was upbeat and really emphasised the style and pace of the show to the listener. Another technique he used was never to give the listener an opportunity to tune away from his programme. He avoided saying things like 'We'll be back after the break' before he played the ads and at the end of his stint he didn't say 'goodbye' or 'more from me tomorrow', he had a short and friendly handover chat with the next presenter which was followed by a station ident and a piece of music.

If you have access to a microphone and a source of music have a go at talking over the instrumental introduction to a song. Time it first then decide what you are going to say then try it out. If possible record your efforts and listen back. Did it sound right? Was your timing good? Did what you said make sense? Try building up a short programme using music tracks and perhaps writing and reading some local news, weather and travel information; maybe later include a short live interview with someone. Before long you will realise that you are presenting a programme.

INTERVIEWING

In the book *Interviewing for Radio* (Beaman 2000) I say that the interviewer's job is to act as a catalyst and to put the questions the listener would like to ask and the questions the listener ought to ask. A broadcast interview is a basic tool of speech communication and therefore the techniques need to be perfected early in your career.

Interviewing for programmes takes on two forms: interviewing as part of the research process or interviewing as part of a live broadcast or recording for broadcast. In both cases the interview will take place face-to-face in the studio or on location or via the telephone or satellite or remote studio down an ISDN line.

The most satisfactory results seem to come from the face-to-face interview either in the studio or on location using portable recording equipment. The sound quality is usually better and you can maintain eye contact with and read the body language of the interviewee. On-air chat can sound informal and relaxed, in fact some pre-senters rely on this style and encourage their guests to be the same, but when you think about it we don't hear a conversation between two people but one person who is asking the questions and the other who is answering. As an interviewer it is important that you control and stay in charge of the interview. Interviewing style needs to be appropriate to the programme style – is it news-based on a speech station or entertainment on a music station? – and the subject matter.

Here are some thoughts and general guidelines for you to consider, particularly if you have never interviewed before.

Imagine you are preparing then conducting a five minute interview.

Practice makes perfect. Try out your technique on a friend or a member of the family. What will your interview be about? It needs to be very focused – just one topic to be explored in a little depth. You need to interview them about a subject they have knowledge about and can talk about with some enthusiasm. Interview your friend about their favourite music, holiday or sport. Interview a grandparent about their childhood or first job. Your job is to ask the questions that will give the listener an interesting insight into the subject. The answers are more important than the questions, but you will be in control of the outcome so you need to play your part effectively. What is the one question you must ask if you had the chance to ask only one? This is your starting point. It is the most important question and should be the one the listener would want you to ask. Other questions should then follow naturally based on the reply you get. This means you should listen to what your interviewee says rather than following a preprepared list of questions which the listener will be able to tell you are reading from. It is best not to write out questions in full, but keep a list in note form to jog your memory. For example you may ask your interviewee to describe to you their first day at work as a starting question then on your notepad you may have written down the words 'duties', 'pay', 'work mates', 'bosses and unions' and 'how spend first week's wages'. You can then find words to convert these notes into spontaneous-sounding and correctly placed questions during the interview. Other or alternative questions may spring to mind based on the answers you are getting so be prepared to be flexible and drop questions or change the order you had planned.

Keep your questions short and simple. Resist the temptation to start one question with another such as 'Can I start by asking you . . .?' Ask your question then stay quiet and don't feel you have to give verbal responses to what the interviewee says like 'yes, I see' or 'OK' as these can be irritating and distracting for the listener. Interruptions by the interviewer are only really effective if you are challenging what they are saying. Encourage the speaker with a simple nod and smile while maintaining eye contact.

Once you have interviewed a number of friendly guinea pigs you should try out your skills on relative strangers – a local shopkeeper, vicar or priest, or librarian.

Eventually you will be face-to-face with your first real stranger who comes to the studio to be interviewed for a programme.

EDITING

Not all radio is live: some items even whole programmes will be pre-recorded and then broadcast. The invention of recording equipment in the early 1890s and the development of plastic tape in the 1930s enabled speech, music and sounds to be recorded and consequently edited. It is at the editing stage that you start to hear the finished shape and structure of the programme. Editing should be seen as part of the creativity of production.

In radio in order to tell a story to the listener effectively and efficiently we edit material to shorten its length to fit into a time slot, to remove unwanted material like retakes or mistakes and to change the order in which the material was recorded. This involves editing raw material that will form the component parts of the piece and editing the programme as a whole once it has been recorded. Develop your own system and routines to help speed up the process and to stay in control. Before you begin to edit anything take time to listen through to your raw material and make notes.

The recorded material is downloaded in real time into a computer software program and edited. This is a non-destructive form of editing because you are working on a copy of the original recording and the software also allows you to undo your edits if you change your mind. Concentrate on the material you intend to keep, not that which you intend to discard, and be organised in your editing procedures. A visual representation of the recording can seen on the screen in the form of a sound wave and you listen to the actual sounds via headphones. The mouse is used to highlight sections of the sound waves and they can be deleted or moved to another part of the piece. Rough edit the material first, because you can do the tidying up or fine editing once you have the basic piece in some sort of order. Music and sounds can also be downloaded, edited and then mixed with interview material. Your edit decisions will also be governed by the duration of the slot it has to fit into and how soon your deadline is for completion. Good editors are quick and accurate but that is something that only comes with practice.

Remember to listen to the completed piece while looking away from the screen so that you can concentrate on how it will sound to the radio listener. Listen to the whole piece before and after you broadcast or save it to MD, CD or playout system.

The completed piece is then saved and downloaded into a playout system or storage facility until it is accessed and played out on air.

During a broadcast any edits should be unnoticeable to the listeners: they should not be able to hear the join and the speech rhythms of the original recordings should be maintained by remembering to leave in and use speakers' breaths.

There are also ethical considerations to be borne in mind when you are editing. Any interviewees should have been informed at the time of recording that their contribution would be edited prior to broadcast. It should really go without saying that you should not deliberately or unintentionally change the meaning or intentional of what your interviewee is saying.

GETTING ON WITH IT

So what activities and tasks can be carried out before, during and after the programme?

Before the programme:

- Research – allow plenty of time and effort for this activity.

- Booking guests, equipment etc. – communications skills come to the fore as do efficiency and ensuring definite confirmation.

- Planning – ongoing and involving the whole team but coordinated by a well-organised producer.

- Cue writing – a combined effort between the producer and the presenter.

- Scripting – as above – a combined effort.

- Music selection – by computer if a general music-based or strip programme using a playlist or by producer for use in speech-based features, packages etc., by producer and presenter if it is for a specialist music programme.

During the programme:

- Calling up guests who will be contributing via line or telephone.

There are a number of pieces of studio equipment that come into play during the programme. As well as the mixing desk or panel, CD and MD players there are computer-based systems operated by the presenter or the producer. These do vary from station to station but they all basically do the same job and are similar in design.

The Electronic News Production System (ENPS) is used at the BBC and gives staff access to the latest news text on their own and other stations, daily prospects, allows them to build and store their programme running orders, type up and store scripts and cues and links, and a news alert for urgent messages for those on air.

Radioman, used by parts of the BBC, allows them to build and edit programmes and programme material.

The Broadcast Network Control System (BNCS), which is operated via a touch screen, allows them to receive, answer and store telephone calls and access staff and contributors in outside studios via ISDN lines.

Visual talkback allows the producer in the studio to put messages on a screen during the programme for the presenter to read. This usually includes details about callers, contributors and general updates and reminders

After the programme:

Ask yourself and the rest of the team 'Did that work?' Ask for and give feedback – not criticism. Use expressions like: What I liked . . . We had problems with . . . Could we in future think about . . . We should have more . . . We could have less . . .

Don't get into the 'Good . . . but' syndrome of programme reviewing. Spend just as much time discussing the good things as well as the room for improvements. Learn from each programme, unpack it and then move on to the next programme you have planned ensuring that anything you felt went wrong with the programme doesn't have the opportunity to occur again.

There may be tidying up activities connected to the programme that should be dealt with as soon as possible like contracts, travel expenses, copies of recordings promised to contributors, prizes for the competition winners, completing, submitting and filing of paperwork (or its paperless equivalent) such as music logs, preparation of archive or web site material.

You might like to try to come up with your own idea for a programme for your favourite station. Hopefully you will know the kind of audience it targets.

First decide on the time slot and duration for transmission and if your programme will be live or recorded. Next you should think about what your programme will be about – try to be original rather than simply adapting a programme already on the air. Now think about the format – is it all music or will there be an equal amount of speech; if you are having speech items, what will they be about? Will you be inviting people in for interviews? How about a competition? Will this be a fast-moving show or gently paced and who would you like to present it? The programme will also need a title.

Try to draw up a running order on paper for each of the items and note the duration of each one.

Looking at the running order, can you hear that programme in your head? If it was broadcast on the radio would you want to listen to it?

Now try writing a short snappy billing for a listings magazine that sums up what the listener can expect to hear if they tune in.

5
The production line

Let's examine the specific requirements of a selection of programme types. From this you should be able to work out the roles and contribution made to each by the various members of the programme staff as listed in Chapter 2 and any extra work and other considerations that make be required to build on the basic programme in Chapter 4. You might like to scan across the stations on your radio and identify the different programme types that they are broadcasting.

THE MUSIC PROGRAMME

Many broadcasters dream of becoming a top DJ but few are going to make it. What could be better than your own programme at peak listening time on a national network playing the music you choose?

Presenting a music programme requires more skill than simply introducing a piece of music with 'This is . . .' and back announcing it with 'That was . . .' and in between leaning back and enjoying the music. Have a go yourself: choose a favourite piece of music and think of six different ways you could introduce and back announce it. Then time yourself reading the introductions aloud and then rewrite them so that they would fit into a 10, 20 or 30 second time slot. The music programme presenter will make full use of material and techniques available to them. Timing is as important in music presentation for the DJ as it is for a comedian. Talking over the introductory instrumental segment of a piece of music and stopping before the vocal begins, chasing the fade by talking over the end of the piece as it fades out and segueing and cross-fading one piece of music seamlessly into another are all skills that need practice and a creative streak. The art of the music presenter is about integrating speech and music and making the programme flow.

The presenter or DJ cannot really afford the luxury of simply sitting back and listening to the music they are playing – they do that later in their own time when they're not being paid to entertain the listener. Also they may not actually like the music they are playing – after all the playlist decisions may have been made by someone else and anyway the presenter needs the time as a record is playing and the microphone is closed to set up the next track, select the ads for the next break, check that the newsreader has taken up position in the news booth, welcome their interview guest into the broadcast cubicle and check the microphone levels.

Jo Tyler produced the first programme broadcast by the BBC's 6Music when it was launched in March 2002:

> *Not all the producers who joined 6Music when it started were experienced radio producers. They were chosen for their musical knowledge, enthusiasm for music and experience with the music industry – some had for example managed bands. When it came to the content of programmes we were determined that we would make full and creative use of the music and other archives kept by the BBC.*

The presenter of that first breakfast show was Phill Jupitus, best known as a comedian but also knowledgeable about music, who had previously presented a show on the BBC's London-based radio station GLR, has made regular appearances on a TV music panel game and has directed music videos (a perfect combination, some would argue).

Not all stations play back to back music tracks. Stations like the BBC's 1Extra are very keen to attract audiences for speech programming. This is a challenge for their producers and presenters who need to be creative and imaginative to make programmes that will appeal to an audience who have primarily tuned in for the music output. The same sort of challenge faced Radio 1 when it wanted to provide its listeners with an acceptable form of news. It developed the hugely popular *Newsbeat* which had all the authority of BBC news but with the pace and stories that appealed to a young audience who would normally turn off.

One thing that music fans do like to hear on the radio is interviews with musicians. The performers and their record labels are also usually keen to take part as it raises their profile and helps promote their music on record and live appearances. However, after a few successive appearances on a string of stations the band members quickly become bored with being asked the same questions and can sound flat on air. Unfortunately some interviews fail because the interviewer has a 'groupie' approach to asking the questions and forgets about what the listener should be hearing, or because of the marketing agenda the interview can end up being just another sales pitch.

Matt Horne, who is a regular music programme presenter and Student Radio Award winner, thinks it is up to the presenter/interviewer to put in the work to be taken seriously:

> *You need to research even the smallest name band properly and demonstrate that you have a brain and a real interest in their music.*

Interviewing in the studio is best as location interviews especially before or after sound checks at venues tend to be full of interruptions and extraneous noise making it hard for everyone to focus and concentrate. I tend to get them to talk about particular tracks which I then play, performing, touring and later throw in a few human interest questions – the sort of questions the fan would want to ask for themselves if they were in the studio.

Sarah Urban finds interviewing new bands particularly challenging:

Because of their inexperience new bands tend to mumble or show off when they are in front of a microphone which is different to the arrogance of some of those who have been around for a while. Some think they are bigger than they really are; for example, if you ask them how they got together they seem to think everyone should already know that. To help avoid these problems you need a proper warm-up session before the broadcast to help build up confidence and some sort of relationship with each other.

Matt and Sarah have both been involved in running student and RSL stations and sum up some of the mistakes that are common amongst new presenters or DJs on music programmes:

It is easy to forget to lower the music to the proper level when you are doing voice-overs and forgetting to bring it back up again. Watching levels generally seems to take them a bit of time to get used to. In the same way leaving faders open once a track has finished and you suddenly hear the next track on the CD playing – it sounds really amateurish – or leaving dead air at the end of a track before they open their mic to speak rather than getting into the practice of opening it slightly early so you can jump straight in at the end. Also some tend to want to just play their favourite tracks on show after show or stick to just one style of music which can be boring for the general audience.

Some music programmes invite music requests or suggestions from their listeners. This can cause problems if the same favourite tracks are asked for over and over again or it can be an opportunity for the all-important listener to make a positive contribution and a station or programme to develop new music and play lists. Listeners to music programmes hope to hear not only the familiar but also be excited by something new. This is particularly important to those who like to download their own music; they only listen to the radio in the hope of hearing something new. If they hear a track from a band that are new to them on the radio and like their sound they will begin searching for other tracks and it can help them decide if they will buy their CDs.

Which tracks to play and which tracks not to play are often decided by the Head of Music on a station and their presenters at regular playlist meetings. The playlists contain the core music, but not all the tracks, the station will play during their peak listening hours. Matt Horne has had experience of one technique employed by his team:

> The idea is not to name the performer but to just play the track and if it receives general approval it gets included. The thinking behind this is to do away with preconceived ideas. This means that a musician who is not usually featured by the station gets airtime because the team liked the track and the decision to include it was based on musical quality, not on the personality or image of the performer.

Stations will draw up 'A' and 'B' playlist selections that determine when and how often the chosen music will be aired. The idea is to provide a consistent station sound for the listener and the presenter choices are expected to adhere strictly to the songs in the playlist when they are planning their programmes. The software will allow them to see what is on offer in various categories such as date, name of performer, male or female vocal, group or solo artiste, song title, ballad or rocker, instrumental and even duration so that the programme can be built and balanced. This method can also help avoid clashes in strip programming ensuring that the same track isn't played in successive shows. They will then load the selections into the scheduling software ready to play on air. This software will also take care of music logging for copyright returns. On other stations the producers and presenters, particularly on specialist music shows, are expected to make the selections for their programmes based on an understanding of the general music policy and order up the tracks from the gram library.

Music stations and programmes will usually be defined and categorised by the music style they choose to play and their audiences determined by that selection. Terms that you will come across include easy listening, country, adult-oriented rock.

THE NEWS PROGRAMME

The format and structure of a news programme may well be established to aid the team of programme makers and journalists involved in its production but because of the nature of news the actual content will ensure that no two editions will sound the same. The news programme gives the station the opportunity to develop and comment on the stories that have been contained in the hourly news bulletins.

Paul Jenner, a broadcast journalist with a BBC local radio station, works on the breakfast show:

> I speak to a variety of people daily on a number of interesting issues, but often there isn't the time to go into great depth due to the deadlines. They're always looming and it's a case of trying to find the most suitable

guest in a reasonable amount of time. That's sometimes a real challenge and there's a sense of satisfaction when you find the right one. Phone-bashing is an inevitable part of what I do and it can be incredibly frustrating at times. Often I will leave several messages to a number of potential guests and then when I think the item will fall down everyone phones back.

The approach to story gathering has changed on local stations. The emphasis was simply to find local stories and local angles on national stories. Now news teams are also looking for particular types of stories for specific slots designed to make the news more relevant to the targeted listener, not just any local person who may have tuned in. So a breakfast show will be designed to contain not only a top or important local story and a local angled national story but also a 'people' story, a health or consumer story and an entertainment story. As Paul Jenner explains, the focus on the audience is more distinct:

To help targeting BBC local radio stations have two theoretical model listeners called 'Dave and Sue' and we're encouraged to think about their lifestyle and activity when planning output. In many respects this follows a similar system which has spread across many commercial station groups. When I used to work for 2-TenFM in Reading (part of GCap) we used to model our stories and the way we told them to 'Nicola from Northants'.

Breakfast shows produced by news staff on both ILR and BBC local stations will contain the same sort of material but feature more time checks, newspaper reviews, regular news headlines and travel updates. They are aware that many in their audience will probably listen to a small part of the whole programme. A typical format on a BBC local station in the morning would be spread over three hours from six until nine with some material repeated in the separate hours.

This is the hour between 7 and 8 am on 18 May 2005 as I heard it on BBC Southern Counties Radio.

0700	News, sport, travel and weather
0707	Live line interview update on local crime story that had been receiving national coverage
0709	Consumer report package provided by GNS
0715	News headlines
0718	Talk up for mid-morning programme
0719	Travel news
0720	Live studio interview with representative from Surrey Fire and Rescue with topical safety warning about tea-light candles
0725	Live phone interview with writer for TV listings magazine about reality TV

0730   News, travel and weather
0735   Live studio interview about a preservation society and their search for the owner of a local bridge
0739   Live telephone interview with music event organiser
0745   News headlines
0746   Talk up for drivetime programme
0747   Sport
0751   Travel
0753   Repeat of 0720 interview
0800   News, sport, travel and weather

As another example let's look at the running order of a typical half-an-hour news programme on an independent local radio station.

This is a double-headed drivetime programme using topical material produced locally and gleaned national stories from IRN. The stories will be told using a range of modes of delivery – written copy and cues, interviews (live or recorded), live two-ways, recorded or voice-pieces, recorded wraps, vox pops and packages. At this time of day cues will often contain time checks and certainly station branding.

1800   Menu. Read over station news programme music bed. As well as introducing the two presenters it features flip-flop presentation of the top three news story headlines with, when possible, illustrative audio clips
1801   Top story 1. Main news item in detail as listed in the menu. Flip-flop cue
1803   Bulletin. A three minute round-up of the rest of the day's news including audio clips. Again flip-flop presentation over a station music bed
1806   Top Story 2. Second main story listed in the menu. Flip-flop cue
1808   Promote ahead to travel news, weather update and sport. Presenter 1 reads
1809   Showbiz or lightweight story with audio clips. Presenter 2 reads cue
1811   Headlines and promote other stories still to come. Presenter 1 reads
1812   Break for advertisements
1814   Travel news. Flip-flop presentation over music bed.
1816   Top story 3. Main news item in detail as listed in menu. Flip-flop cue
1818   Sports news. Presenter 2 links to sports reporter who presents with audio clips
1820   Local story. 1 Flip-flop cue
1822   Business news. Presenter 1 reads
1824   Local story 2. Flip-flop cue
1826   Entertainment guide. Local events. Prepared package. Presenter 2 links to reporter who presents
1828   Weather and travel news. Flip-flop
1829   Closing headlines. Flip-flop presentation over music bed
1830   End

Notice the mixture of material contained within the programme. Those stories could contain hard news angles and topics and others lightweight or entertainment news, making it quite a challenge for the presenters. Double-headed presentation of a programme also offers its own challenges. There must be a reason for paying two presenters: they should both have a specific role to play and the chemistry between them must be right.

A station may for example employ a male and a female combination to give a gender balance not only in presence but also in approach and angle to the content and both can contribute to and lead discussions by reflecting differing and common attitudes to topics.

This format is similar to one you might hear on a BBC local station and it is a large concentration of speech for a station where the output is mostly music-based. It is aimed at an audience either busy at home or travelling homewards.

Newsroom staff in BBC and commercial stations also produce news-based programmes in the form of 'specials' or mini-documentaries at the start or culmination of a big local story, making use of material collected and archived over time.

THE MAGAZINE PROGRAMME

Take a look at the shelves of any newsagents and you find a baffling array of magazines aimed at particular groups with general or specialist interests. There are women's magazines containing stories and features about subjects that the publishers believe will be of general interest to their target audience and there are specialist magazines that focus on one subject area – dogs, gardening, cars, computers – and trade magazines. As you will see if you reach for a TV and radio listings magazine radio has its own equivalent versions ranging from music, science, the arts and so on in the form of programmes. These programmes like their print equivalents have target audiences, an identity and appropriate content and style of presentation. Instead of a cover the radio version may have a signature tune and certainly a regular presenter to front the programme. There is a spoken menu as a radio equivalent to a magazine index page, often illustrated with short clips or extracts from the items coming up later in the programme to act as tasters and attract the listener's attention. At the end of the programme there will sometimes be a form of trailing ahead to the next edition to encourage the listener to listen again.

The content, structure and running order of the magazine programme are as crucial to the success of the programme as the personality and talent of the presenter. Let's consider a half hour weekly live magazine programme that deals with the subject of travel. Here is a list of the content for our fictional programme. The durations include cues, links and back announcements to total 29 minutes – the balance will be taken up with the programme introduction and closing. Which order would you put them in the programme and why? Your decisions will be guided not only by editorial considerations and production values but also the simple logistics of getting live interview guests in and out of the studio. Obviously the best time to do this is when a pre-recorded piece is being played and the studio microphones are off. Bear in mind that the reporter is part of the team and will be au fait with studio routines so could stay in the studio until required for their live slots.

1   A pre-recorded light-hearted feature in the form of an audio diary following two teenagers on a day out in York. (Duration five minutes.) The two teenagers will also be available in the studio for a short live chat after the piece is transmitted. (Duration 2 minutes.)

2   A pre-recorded report from a wheelchair user about access to major tourist attractions at seaside resorts. (Duration five minutes.) Spokespersons from two of the resorts mentioned will be available for a live interview after the piece. One guest will be in the studio with the presenter, the other will be down the line from an outside studio. (Duration five minutes.)

3   Programme reporter has been researching dog-based activity weekends around the UK and is available for a live discussion in the studio. (Duration four minutes.)

4   A pre-recorded piece on a group of writers offering literary tours of Paris. (Duration four minutes.)

5   A live listings round-up of events around the country this weekend from the reporter and presenter. (Duration two minutes.)

6   Live interview with travel expert on latest health warnings issued by the British government to travellers planning a trip to the Far East. (Duration two minutes.)

There is no totally right or wrong answer and decisions will be affected by availability of live guests. For example the travel expert or one of the resort spokespersons may only be available to take part in a certain time slot and the rest of the programme may have to be built around them.

However, in a perfect world I would probably lead with the live interview with the travel expert on the latest health warnings. It is topical and it is always a good idea to get the presenter and the listeners settled in with a studio-based live piece. The guest would be at their microphone opposite the presenter before the programme goes on air so that they can be interviewed directly after the opening menu and the introduction to them has been read by the presenter. During this item the studio producer and the studio manager would be establishing contact with the resort spokesperson waiting in the outside studio link.

I would then follow this with the pre-recorded report on the seaside resorts during which the first guest will be shown out of the studio by the PA and the other resort spokesperson settled into the studio. This is an issue-led piece with a strong story and would have probably been the lead if the health warning story had not arisen. I would also ask the other reporter who will be reporting on activity weekends to join the presenter around the table in the studio. After the feature the presenter would have a conversation on the issues raised with the two resort spokespersons. The guest in the studio will need to wear headphones so that they can hear what is being said by the contributor speaking down the line.

This would be followed by the live conversation with the second reporter on activity holidays. The studio guest could stay in the studio while this is going on.

Next would be the pre-recorded piece from the teenagers in York during which the guest and the reporter would leave the studio and be replaced by the teenagers ready for their live chat.

This would be followed by the recording about Paris during which the two guests would leave and the reporter would return for the live listings segment with the presenter. This final live segment allows for some programme flexibility. It can be extended or curtailed as required and if necessary moved to a different place in the running order if there is a problem.

So the running order would show where the items would fit into the programme and the timings would fit into the 11.30 am–midday slot allocated for the programme.

Start time	Content	Source	Duration	End time
11.30.00	Greeting and menu	Live	0'30"	11.30.30
11.30.30	Health interview	Live	2'00"	11.32.30
11.32.30	Resort report	Recording	5'00"	11.37.30
11.37.30	Resort interviews	Live	5'00"	11.42.30
11.42.30	Dog activity report	Live	4'00"	11.46.30
11.46.30	York report	Recording	5'00"	11.51.30
11.51.30	York interview	Live	2'00"	11.53.30
11.53.30	Paris report	Recording	4'00"	11.57.30
11.57.30	Listings	Live	2'00"	11.59.30
11.59.30	Close & trail ahead	Live	0'30"	12.00.00

Think about how you would cope and what you would do if you were the studio producer on this programme and the first of the live interviews overran its allotted time slot. What would you do if one of the guests for the discussion about resorts didn't show because they were caught in traffic on the way to the studio? All good producers have a standby recorded piece based on a timeless subject with them in the studio – what would yours be about for this travel programme? Based on the items listed have a go at writing the opening menu for the presenter that will grab the listener's attention and make them want to listen to the whole programme. Do you think the running order would be affected if one of your live interviewees or reporter on one of your recorded items was a well-known personality or celebrity? If so, would you put them at the start of the programme where traditionally the strongest story would be chosen to lead or at the end so that the listener will stay throughout the programme to hear the celebrity at the end? Can you try and come up with some general questions to put to the guest who will be talking about a health scare in the Far East? Try writing a short trail for the programme that could be read during another programme earlier in the same day.

THE STRIP PROGRAMME

This is a regular – usually daily – programme that is a mix of live and recorded speech and music items, fronted by a regular presenter or sometimes double-headed. It has a set format to provide a fixed structure and regular items to fulfil audience expectations. Unlike sequence programmes, each of which is structured to have a particular and individual identity, strip programmes flow seamlessly and hand over from one programme presenter to another with a consistent sound.

Let's take as an example the weekday mid-morning programme (9 am–1 pm) on a BBC local radio station – BBC Southern Counties based in Guildford. The presenter is Tony Fisher and the producer Gurindar Barar. It is billed as 'topical entertainment, conversation and information'.

During the programme the presenter not only speaks to the listener from the cubicle but also operates the broadcast desk faders that control the microphones, CD and MD players, and other sound sources. The producer and guests waiting to join the presenter on air are all in a studio away from the live microphones. The presenter in the broadcast cubicle can communicate with them all through the soundproof window that separates them via a talkback system. The producer can answer the calls from listeners and set up the line contributors like the weather and travel centres from this area and transfer them into the cubicle for the presenter to put them on air at the appropriate time. Listeners are encouraged to email directly to the presenter in the studio to be read as required.

This is a long stint for the presenter and not all the content is planned or fixed ahead of the broadcast. Presenter Tony Fisher says,

> Flexibility is the key to a successful programme and when you are on air for four hours a strong bladder. We also like the unexpected – we have a slot called 'The Long Shot' where we ask people to contact us before the end of the programme if they've had a specific and random experience like being in a band that had a Top 40 hit in the 1970s, cycled around the world or some other unlikely experience – it's risky because what are the chances of someone listening at that particular time who had that particular chosen

experience and is prepared to ring in. We've often been surprised and had some great interviews.

Gaps in the schedule are left to enable the programme to respond to breaking news, developing stories and general topicality. Material is slotted into the running order well in advance, the day before, the hour or so before the programme begins and during its four hour run.

Everyone involved in the programme is very calm during the broadcast, which is the way it should be according to producer Gurindar Barar:

If the programme is well prepared and organised so that everyone knows what they should be doing and how to do it and when then there should be no need to rush around or panic or for the producer to spend all their time on the talkback to their presenter.

The first hour contains about four or five pieces of music selected from the station's playlist, a light-hearted competition with the presenters of the previous programmes and then phone-callers and emailers are invited to respond with their comments on the Topic of the Day (e.g. on a day of travel chaos on the local roads they are invited to give examples of bad driving they have encountered). There is Feature of the Day on a wide range of subjects from the hard news to less serious, but again where listeners are also invited to contribute their experiences and opinions. This will have been trailed in advance and some contributions recorded.

Interactivity is a key contribution that the programme has encouraged and the listeners expect to be able to participate.

The second hour will continue to expect listener contributions but guests will be talking with the presenter during fixed slots like Talking Point, which is news or current affairs-based, where the guest could be a journalist, critic or participant.

The third hour includes Sound Advice where one of a team of experts will answer questions and discuss stories in the news about their particular area e.g. buying and using personal computers, and the Helpline where the presenter will interview a local representative from an organisation looking for help in some form or another, for example volunteers to help with a countryside project. This would have been set up with the assistance of the station's helpline coordinator.

The final hour sees more phone calls from listeners, another competition and a live interview with the Guest of the Day. The guest will interviewed about their new book, for example, then subjected to a series of random questions taken from a list of one hundred. The guest chooses a number and the presenter reads out the appropriate question. This is a useful device for getting the interviewee away from the focused topic that they came into the studio to talk about and can reveal some unexpected aspects of their lives or character.

Throughout the programme there is news on the hour, travel, weather and sport updates from regular contributors.

THE FEATURE PROGRAMME AND DOCUMENTARIES

Of all the different radio programme types the radio documentary is perhaps the hardest to define. News producers feel it is an extension of journalism and programme producers will argue it falls into the creative area of storytelling. Some see it purely as a longer form of the feature. It is generally agreed that it is a built or constructed programme giving a factual, authoritative, truthful account and relies on contributions from primary sources or witnesses. It is the presentation of ideas, issues or events told in an imaginative way and shows rather than tells its story. It should develop and reveal its story with texture, colour and the occasional surprise and the production techniques adopted should enhance the story, not obscure it. Documentaries are scripted, recorded and edited programmes, which give you the opportunity to cover plenty of ground economically, but there is a big investment in time because of the production techniques involved. Techniques favoured by documentary programme makers include presenter-led, where narrative links shape the storytelling and lead the listener through the material, fly-on-the-wall with lots of actuality recordings, commentary and audio diary material used to tell the story, montage which uses the seamless flow of interlinking and juxtaposed material and the drama documentary which mixes dramatised sequences and re-enactments with interview and actuality. As with all radio storytelling the documentary relies on the finished product being focused – so decide on your topic, choose an angle and then pick the best approach that will communicate to the audience. Draw out from your contributors their experiences, feelings and opinions and give the piece human interest. Facts and figures and other information are best consolidated into bite-size pieces as part of the presenter's links.

As the work progresses you may become confused by the amount of material you collect, so you need to keep asking yourself 'what is the story I am trying to tell? I usually keep a one sentence summary of the project pinned to the wall and look at it regularly to remind myself and stay focused. Whatever your programme is going to be about and however you intend to tell your story you need to be pragmatic. Don't let the idea become so over ambitious that it becomes unachievable. Spend more of your time on finding the best contributors, collecting quality material and preparing a strong script.

The case study programme in Chapter 6 is that of a feature programme. It is a considered and creative piece of work that makes use of a wide range of knowledge and skills. Not all feature programmes need to be quite so complex. A programme that uses a single extended interview with a film director could use the questions and answers of the interview and links from the interviewer to summarise or change the subject area. The producer would also want to include, if possible, some short extracts from the director's films. This approach is not sufficient for the programme to be called a documentary but it is certainly a feature programme.

Keeping down the costs of making a programme without losing quality or compromising on content is something that regularly challenges producers. One thing to consider is when the presenter needs be involved in the process. For a documentary feature programme I made for BBC Radio 4 which would include collecting interview material on location in several parts of the UK I decided it would be too expensive for the celebrity presenter to be involved in the interview process in the accepted way. It would take about two or more weeks of time-consuming travelling and intense recording, involving as well as his fee the extra hotel and other subsistence expenses. I travelled to the interviews as a representative of the presenter and recorded them, bearing in mind that I would be editing out my contribution and in such a way that the listener would not be aware of the presenter's absence. Each of the items were packaged together in montages and sent to the presenter to listen to and write his links around them. Then it was just a case of bringing the presenter to the studio to record his contribution telling the story and playing in the illustrative montages at the appropriate points in the script. The programme was made in the most economic way possible. The finished product was still honest: we did not insert the presenter's voice asking the questions artificially or imply in the links that he was present at the interviews but the listener still felt the interviewees were speaking directly to them. The interviewer is after all the catalyst and the conduit for the interviewee to communicate with the listener, and the presenter is responsible for the storytelling and flow of the narrative.

Let's imagine you have been asked or you have decided to make a programme about the role of the electric guitar in popular music for a music station. Assuming your fee and the budget have been sorted how would you go about it? Map out a plan of campaign. Jot down thoughts, phrases and impressions, topics, areas to visit, people to talk to. How long must the programme be? Do you know the audience profile of the station? When will it be broadcast? What is the deadline for delivery?

Once you have the answers you need to start work. Have you decided on and booked a presenter? A DJ with a high profile and acknowledged musical knowledge or a commentator on the music industry who writes for a music magazine or the author of a book on the subject – which would you choose? Have you found and booked a studio and technical staff?

You need to read the appropriate books, specialist magazines and web sites to find out as much as you can about the electric guitar. Its history, how and where they are designed and manufactured and where they are sold. You need to find out the classic makes and the top exponents in the art of playing them. Which are considered to be the seminal performances that demonstrate the essence of the electric guitar? Are they available on commercial recordings?

You should be looking for potential contributors who you can interview for your programme. Think about this pragmatically bearing in mind the budget (will it allow for overseas travel?). Are they easy to contact? Do you have any names in your contacts book? Be prepared to compromise on who you would like to have on your programme and who you can get for your programme. Obviously you'll want to interview musicians, but consider also music journalists, critics, academics, authors, manufacturers, record producers, music shop owners and DJs. If you make contact with a potential contributor who says they will get back to you and never does, keep trying them but set yourself a deadline and if you haven't confirmed when and where you can interview them don't waste time, just find an alternative. Don't wait until you have fixed up all your interviewees to start interviewing: remember you have nothing to work with unless you have some recorded material.

The programme subject matter will give you plenty of opportunities to use illustrative material in the form of music tracks, demonstrations of models and techniques and archive.

The structure of the programme – the process by which it tells its story – will be guided by what the contributors have to say and the links which will signpost and progress the narrative. You might want to divide up the programme material into smaller sections or groupings to make it easier to construct; for example in our guitar programme 'scene set', 'the early days', 'technical developments', 'guitar heroes', 'great performances', 'the future'.

The successful programme sounds whole and complete. It depends on getting credible interviews, writing an accessible script, attractive presentation and consistent production.

Once you have decided on the topic, think about the angle and then the mode of delivery. Then to produce a programme you need to:

- Search – find appropriate facts and figures. Identify potential contributors. Find illustrative material to enhance the storytelling and make the programme radiogenic.

- Fix – arrange to interview contributors in the studio or better still in an appropriate location. You should warn contributors that although you are interviewing them what they say will be edited and that there is no guarantee that you will use the material. Look for opportunities to record material beyond the set interviews and obvious sound effects. Decide beforehand the questions you want answering that will supply the information you need to impart in the programme. Think about how the interview will fit into the piece as a whole and the contribution you hope it will make. Will you interview with the intention of excluding your questions from the final piece?

- Collect – record the interview material and access music tracks etc.

- Edit – start the editing process by making notes of what you think are the best bits and the durations, but don't start editing the audio until you have all your interviews as this will affect your editorial decisions and help you choose clips and see where there may be some gaps you will need to fill. Remember that material that doesn't make it into the final clip selection could be used as a base or stimulus for your written links.

- Script – once you have your interview clips in the order you feel they could be used to tell the story and have decided which musical tracks you are going to use then you should be able to pre-hear the finished programme in your head. It helps if you know how you want the programme to start and end, then all you have to worry about is how to take the listener from A to B. You now need to commit the running order to paper and also write the links for the presenter that will stick the whole narrative together. Check that you have enough material to fill the time allocated to the programme. Ensure that you have all your facts correct – if in doubt ask someone to read through the script to see if they feel there are any inaccuracies – watch out for dates, pronunciation of names of people and places in particular. Is the piece focused on the story and does it tell it clearly but creatively? Will the programme just tell its story or preferably show its story to the listener?

- Construct – armed with the script, clips, music tracks and presenter you can head to the studio and record your programme.

- Edit (2) – there are bound to be retakes, mistakes etc. that will need to be trimmed out and maybe even some slight remixing to change the duration of the piece.

- Listen – do not think that when you have completed the last edit the programme is ready. Listen through to the whole programme on loudspeakers with the script at your elbow. Check for missed edits, technical hiccups and the duration but above all listen to how it sounds. Is this the piece you were asked to produce? Does it sound good? Listen to it again the next day and allow others to listen and give you their thoughts.

- Submit – hand over your creation to its new parents together with all the proper paperwork, preferably ahead of schedule so that they can return it to you if they find fault. Remember to keep a copy for yourself.

THE DISCUSSION PROGRAMME

A discussion programme usually takes place at a round table in a studio. Each of the participants will be seated at their own microphone. Only the presenter will need to wear headphones so that they can receive instructions from the producer. The presenter will also need to be able to see a clock. Most studios will have different coloured wind-shields on each of the microphones to help the studio operators identify the speakers and open and close their microphones from the control room as required.

Crucial to the success of a discussion programme are the choice of chairperson and participants. It should be decided early on in the planning stages as to who this will be and whether they will be expected to participate by voicing their own opinions and sharing their own experiences or to remain neutral and perhaps act as devil's advocate during the debate. The chairperson needs to be fully briefed about the topic under discussion and about the status, role and opinions of the contributors to enable them to successfully orchestrate the discussion. The contributors should hold a variety of individual views and in order to help the listener and avoid confusion try to cast voices that are easily distinguishable. To this end and to make the debate manageable limit the number of contributors: three plus the chairperson is about right in most cases. Sometimes it happens that not all the contributors will be around the table in the studio; for a variety of reasons you may have one linked via line to another studio or in extreme cases on the telephone. It is important that this contrib-utor is not forgotten in the heat of debate by the chair or the other participants.

When you book and confirm your speakers for the discussion make sure everyone is briefed and understands what the discussion will be about, who else will be taking part and the views that they will represent. It is possible that someone will refuse or object to sharing a platform with another of your guests, in which case you must decide whether to try and get them to change their minds or look for another contributor. Asking them if they have any suggestions for an alternative with similar views, experience, knowledge and so on may just be enough for them to agree reluctantly to participate after all. Don't try and hide anything in the hope of avoid-ing this situation or enlivening the interview when they meet on air. Chances are someone will cry foul and your reputation and that of the programme and the station will be sullied.

Formats and structures of these kinds of programmes do vary. Some producers like to use pre-recorded material like vox pops, archive or actuality to kick start the subject under discussion, others prefer a detailed introduction from the chairperson who will then introduce the participants to the listener. Sometimes each speaker will be invited to briefly summarise their viewpoint on the topic. This can help establish the contrasting views in the mind of the listener. Hopefully the participants will have been briefed during the research stage of the production as to who they will be facing across the table. They will have also been advised about the procedures (like putting up their hand if they want to speak) and any technical information they may need to know (like what the red light in the studio means and if they will need to wear headphones).

The chairperson should use questions to the participants to elicit more detailed opinions and allow free discussion between them. It may be necessary for the chair to ask for clarification, ask another speaker for their views, or step in if everyone is speaking at the same time, but generally they are there to ensure that all the speakers get a fair opportunity to have their say and keep an eye on the clock. To help the listener to follow the arguments the chairperson should always make a point of naming each participant before they speak and including their name when putting a question to them.

The discussion programme relies heavily on the abilities of the chairperson who, if they have been well briefed and rehearsed, should be left to get on with their job. The producer who may be on the other side of the glass during the broadcast or recording should use talkback to the chairperson only if it is urgent and should keep the message brief to avoid causing too much of a distraction.

If you are in the chair be positive in your control of the discussion and encouragement to the participants. Indicate who you want to speak next in the discussion by pointing at them and saying their name. This sends a signal to the others to remain quiet and tells the listener whose voice they are hearing. Show an interest in what is being said by active listening – a nod of the head, a smile. Avoid having more than one person speaking at once, which can be confusing for the listener, by holding up your hand, palm towards the person you would like to be quiet, and pointing at the person who should speak.

There can be a temptation, which should be resisted, to allow more airtime to the best performer; the one who is calm and collected, who sounds sensible and offers reasonable arguments. This is not in the interest of good listening. Encourage and cajole responses and contributions from all your guests. If you have a dominant speaker try breaking in at an appropriate point by saying 'That's an interesting point . . .' or 'You mentioned that . . .' and then once you have control of the microphone turn to another guest and ask 'What do you think of that argument?' or 'I would imagine that's a view you also hold?' The same technique can be used to interrupt a speaker who may be rambling or digressing. This will re-establish your control over the discussion, achieve a polite interruption that avoids embarrassment to the speaker, and moves the debate on.

The way the programme ends is also important. There is nothing worse than a programme that sounds ragged and un-produced at its close, unless it's one that has simply run out of steam and fizzles out. This can be done in a variety of ways. The easiest is to have a written piece of script that contains some closing remarks and a thank you to the guest speakers who should be named. It may also contain details of the web site where the listener can access further information about the programme and indeed listen to it again. Whatever the closing link contains it should be timed so that the reader knows in advance how much air time it will take up and know when they should begin reading it. The chair could allow time for each of the participants to make one last point or perhaps even summarise or make a final point themselves before thanking and naming the speakers. Whatever the method used, the closing sequence should be scripted and planned with as much care as the opening to ensure an efficient and professional-sounding positive ending to the programme.

THE PHONE-IN PROGRAMME

Phone-in programmes featuring the voices of members of the public began in Britain in 1968 on BBC local radio. They established an interactive open line for listeners to phone in their music requests or participate in competitions and gradually developed a swap-shop for listeners who wanted to exchange unwanted items. Others followed suit and encouraged those early rather wary callers to put questions to a studio guest – a local council official or local expert – or simply chat with the presenter of the programme about a lightweight topic of the day. The content or subjects under discussion would vary according to the time of day or current affairs. The 'agony aunt' or 'open line' where callers could discuss almost anything was often used to fill late night schedules. These early experiments were not officially approved by BBC bosses in London but by 1970 national radio took up on the idea with *It's Your Line*, hosted by Robin Day. Commercial radio flirted with the use of 'shock-jocks' who were deliberately rude or gave short shrift to their callers, however, after a short but interesting relationship they went out of favour.

Shingler and Wieringa (1998: 125) assert that a caller to a station is not an isolated voice but probably speaks for a number of listeners who are tuned in to the pro-gramme. Indeed it is probably safe to say that if one caller states an opinion that opinion will be shared by at least ten of your listeners who have not phoned in.

When a listener calls into the station phone-in number they are connected to the producer of the programme who will chat with them to establish their take on the subject under discussion, what they want to say and how they are likely to come across on air. The caller's number is noted and they are called back when the producer needs them to be on air. This means the caller isn't left hanging on and the station pays for the call. It is also another check that this is a bona fide caller. Once contact is established the caller is put on hold and can hear the programme as it is being broadcast down their phone line. The caller's details are put on the visual talkback for the presenter who then switches them to the studio and puts them on air. Computer systems like BNCS and PhoneBox are specially designed for radio phone-ins and allow the producer to store the caller's number. They can even check if and when they have contributed before and keep notes about the quality of the contribution.

Phone-ins do have their downsides. They can attract those who like to complain and those unfortunates who have nothing else in their lives and need an outlet for their banal ramblings which some stations provide. Phone-ins can be dull, irritating and sometimes offensive unless they are well thought out and planned, have a purpose and role in the general output and are intelligently produced with the listeners, not just the callers, needs in mind. There have been, and there still are, good phone-ins. Nick Ross on BBC Radio 4 requested that callers who had experience or specialist knowledge about the topic to call in and presenter Brian Hayes on LBC and BBC networks always insisted that callers to his programme should have something to say that would add something to the debate and were prepared to have their opinions challenged and not to just phone in for a rant. The result was that as a listener you felt you had learnt something from their on-air contributions. Simon Fanshawe on his BBC Five Live *Living Soap* staged his phone-in so that he took the same half dozen callers each week and talked to them about what was going on in their lives. The result was continuity and a feeling of inclusion and empathy with the callers. So it is obvious that you should not underestimate the importance of the initial filtering of callers by the producer to get the right material to give the programme balance and structure. There can also be a dilemma if the calls are not coming in as thick and fast as you would hope. Do you put through a caller simply because there is no one else available?

The producer can also help keep the programme moving at a proper pace by gleaning information from the caller that can be passed on to the presenter via the visual talkback so that they give the listener some background information about the caller's query or opinion and don't waste valuable airtime with basics or minutiae but move on to expressing their views or discussing the issue. For example: 'Our next caller is John who has been involved in raising public awareness about the campaign. You got involved because of an incident that happened to you John so how do you think the system should change?'

If a caller disappears between calling in and getting on air all the presenter can do is say something like. 'We seem to have lost contact with Jack, let's hope we can talk to him later. In the meantime Mary has called in with an idea you might like. . . .'

At the end of the programme resist the temptation to 'squeeze in one final quick caller'. It will probably end up sounding rushed or the caller long-winded or flustered and the programme will end untidily. It is better to end slightly early with a summary, an email contribution or two and remember to thank all the callers and apologise to those who you did not have time to include in the programme.

When thinking about broadcasting a phone-in programme bear in mind the following:

- Are there good and bad times of the day or even the year to hold a phone-in? Are there, for example, likely to be more listeners at home during the colder months and are you less likely to get callers in the early evening compared with late at night?

- If you are choosing a subject for discussion does it have wide listener appeal? Does the taster at the start of the programme really fire their interest and imagination?

- If you intend to use a guest speaker in the studio are they the best person for the job? Can they cope with the unpredictability of the callers?

Trail ahead your programme so that you recruit some of your callers in advance. Callers will start phoning in once the programme is on air and they have heard what others have to say, how they were treated and the sort of responses they were given by you and your guest.

If you don't have any callers lined up before the programme starts it may be some time before it really takes off. Producers I know who have been in this situation usually have the numbers of a couple of friendly regulars they can call who can be trusted to put an appropriate question or make a sensible remark on air to get things moving.

Encourage emails from listeners so that the presenter can read them out. The presenter should also have some relevant questions, comments and research they can draw on if things slow down.

The presenter can ask questions of a guest but be careful as a caller may be just picking up the phone and dialling the studio to ask the very question that has just been asked by the presenter.

If they are alone on air can your presenter handle callers to them with confidence, especially if they are taking calls on highly contentious issues or acting as devil's advocate?

Make sure your presenter knows how to react and respond to listeners who use bad language, say something potentially libellous or make remarks that offend good taste.

Late night phone-in programmes covering controversial subjects are likely to be the source of any problems for the station. If complaints are made and upheld then stations can face hefty fines and may be required to broadcast statements on the regulator's findings several times a day for a week. You can see from the cases featured in the Ofcom Broadcast Bulletins (available at www.ofcom.org.uk) that on rare occasions even the most experienced and long-serving hosts can fall into what is referred to as careless and unauthorised broadcasting by making spur of the moment comments that end up being summarised as unacceptable and potentially harmful.

During Ofcom's investigation the licensee initiated disciplinary procedures against the presenter which eventually resulted in his dismissal. The licensee also said it had put in place new compliance procedures to ensure such a situation does not occur again.

Ofcom Broadcast Bulletin no. 50

Presenters can air their own views – but not emphatically and continuously over the top of callers in a manner that did not allow appropriate and adequate response from others as required by the News and Current Affairs Code.

Ofcom Broadcast Bulletin no. 50

Late night call-in shows have been the making and breaking of broadcasting careers and often stories relating to them hit the headlines. I remember back in the 1970s being enthralled to hear a caller to a Birmingham radio station phone-in informing the presenter that he was on his way to commit suicide. The presenter kept him talking while another member of the team called the police and directed them to the concourse of New Street station. Listeners could quite clearly hear station announcements about departing trains in the background during the call. Eventually after a number of tension-filled minutes police officers arrived at the railway station call box from where he was phoning and gently persuaded him to go along with them for a chat.

More recently the *Daily Telegraph* (7 January 2006) reported how Pete Price, a presenter on Magic FM in Liverpool, abandoned his radio show and rushed off in a taxi to the home of a listener who had collapsed while taking part in his late night phone-in. Another member of the team played music during his absence from the microphone.

THE OUTSIDE BROADCAST PROGRAMME

The first OB transmitted in the UK was by the BBC in 1923 and was a performance of *The Magic Flute* from the opera house at Covent Garden. An ambitious project for a broadcaster's first attempt at something new, but it obviously went well as OBs quickly became a regular feature of radio broadcasts. They add excitement, immediacy, freshness and a sense of danger to the mainly studio-based output of stations. Some of the classic broadcasts have been OBs – sporting events, state funerals and royal weddings.

Of all the different forms of broadcast programmes the outside broadcast rig is perhaps the one that relies most on careful planning. Too many unexpected things can happen and too many things can go wrong to risk any mishaps that could be seen as lack of forethought in planning or detail.

There may be permissions to be sought from local authorities or site owners, equipment and broadcast lines to be booked, risk assessment procedures to be followed and staffing to be decided before you even start thinking about contributors and scripts. The amount of extra preparation, organisation and communication will depend on the complexity of the broadcast. An all day Roadshow at the seaside with musicians playing live in front of an audience? Coverage of a football match with live commentary? Inserts from street party celebrations into a studio-based programme?

At one BBC local station where I worked, the mid-morning programme would stage an outside broadcast once a month from a listener's home. We didn't just turn up – listeners were asked to write in and describe their home, neighbours and town or village and explain why they would like us to broadcast live from their house, trailing microphone cables all over the drive and generally disrupting their lives for the morning. Once the engineers had checked that we could get a strong signal back to the studio via the radio car from the location the content of the programme was planned. Each programme would feature interviews with the host listener, family members and neighbours in the sitting room. We usually managed to take along a star guest too who we were planning to interview that week, for example an actor appearing in repertory at the local theatre or a musician on tour. There would be a regular cookery spot in the kitchen and our horticultural expert offering advice from the garden and sometimes even tips on car maintenance in the garage. The presenter would be live from the house assisted by an engineer, a technical operator would be looking after the mixing desk back in the studio playing in the music tracks, jingles, news studio etc. and prepared to take over with a studio-based programme if contact with the house should be lost. This usually entailed having lots of music tracks and programme trails to play and what's-ons to read out.

This particular OB used the radio car which was equipped to transmit the signal from the house to a receiver usually housed at one of the station's transmitter sites, then on to the studio where it would be fed through the studio desk and back to all the transmitters and broadcast to the listener. Station radio cars are still in use along with buses and satellite vans but with the use of mobile phone technology it is possible for a reporter to take along a portable unit (e.g. Matrix) and broadcast a technically high quality signal from a site which may be inaccessible for a vehicle. For example a reporter sent to cover a major road traffic incident may find it difficult to drive to its location because of blocked or cordoned off areas which restrict vehicular access.

The essential ingredients of a well-planned outside broadcast programme are the same as with any other radio programme – preparation (research, fixing, clearances), organisation (of the team, contributors, schedules, facilities) and communication (between the team, contributors and base) before, during and after the programme.

The radio station you are working for decides that the Saturday lunchtime show 12 noon–3 pm should broadcast live from a small annual flower and produce show. Here is an opportunity to bring the outdoors inside for the listener, to give your programme and station a public appearance and add variety to your programme structure and sound. Public events like these also give you an opportunity to meet the listener and distribute publicity material that raises your profile – like car stickers and programme detail leaflets and handouts. Assuming you have been allocated a budget, a production team made up of a producer to take responsibility for overseeing the project, an engineer or two, a presenter or two, a studio-based technical operator, broadcast assistant (BA) (one to help set up the OB in advance and carry out research and another who can be on site on the day) then make sure that you will be welcome at the event and that the organisers are prepared to cooperate with your coverage. Your engineer will need to confirm that a strong signal can be transmitted and received from the location of the event. If this is unknown territory then it will be necessary to carry out a signal test. If the signal is weak or nonexistent the engineer will need to organise and pay for a landline to be booked, established and tested. Once you get the OK you need to visit the site which at this stage will probably be an open field. If you can arrange it with the organisers it is best if you can be allocated an exhibitor's space to set up your stall. You should be able to negotiate one free of charge – after all you will be publicising the show on air not only on the day but prior to the event during your programme trails. You will also need passes to allow you on and off the site. Arrange your visit on a day when someone will be around to show you where you will be sited, to point out entrance and exit points, where the toilet facilities will be located and where you will be able to park your cars, tell you the times when you will be able to set up and all those other details that you need to know. Now is also a good time to start thinking about conducting a risk assessment exercise to make sure there will no incidents affecting the team or the public and what contingency plans you may have in case of inclement weather. Ask for a programme of events for the day and get a list of the trade stands and exhibitors that will be on site. This information will help you plan and contact potential interview guests for your programme. Importantly find out who will be on the stands in the immediate vicinity and try to ascertain if their presence is likely to interfere with your broadcast. For example if they will be playing music through loudspeakers or giving noisy demonstrations of equipment like lawnmowers you may want to be moved elsewhere. Check out if the loudspeakers for the inevitable public address system will be positioned nearby – you may want to ask the organisers to reconsider. Early in the planning process you need to establish that there is a power supply available and accessible to the broadcast point. While you are on site draw a plan of the showground to remind you of the layout and to show to other members of the team back at base. Don't leave without the contact numbers and addresses of the organisers.

If this was going to be recorded programme for later transmission, say as a special edition of your regular gardening programme, you will need to decide if the programme is to be recorded on site, in which case you will need to book and set up mobile studio facilities, or back in the studio.

The production team now have to decide on a structure for their coverage of the event and the content that will make it into a whole programme. Suggestions could include for example a live interview with the celebrity who has agreed to open the event, interview with the organisers, live demonstrations of horticultural skills by experts invited to the event with the presenter 'having a go' at some of them on air, use of a second presenter who could be a roving microphone around the site interviewing stall holders, exhibitors and the public, interviews and packages that could be pre-recorded earlier in the day before the programme goes on air and played into the broadcast. As much planning and fixing of guests you want to take part should be confirmed as well in advance as is possible.

A running order and timings for the programme can be drawn up and copies of all the documentation including cue sheets etc. prepared for all the team. Alternative programme material should also be prepared for use by the technical operator (TO) in the studio should the programme 'fall off the air'. This could simply be a selection of music but a series of pre-prepared features on a gardening theme would be more appropriate and allow flexibility. Copies of any interviews or packages recorded at the location prior to broadcast could also be sent to the studio in case there is a loss of signal from the outside broadcast. These pieces will also need cue sheets so that the TO can introduce and play them.

Extra recorded material, extra written material and an extra standby guest on site will ensure that the programme will fill its time slot should something go wrong like an expected guest not showing.

Before leaving for the OB make sure everyone has appropriate footwear, clothing for the current and possible inclement weather conditions and any safety equipment they may need like high visibility jackets or vests and hard hats. The mobile phone has proved to be an essential part of an OB communication system between the broadcast team at the event, the studio and the newsroom. Make sure yours is fully charged and that everyone including the TO back at base has your number.

On the day if all goes according to plan everyone involved – the production team, the event organisers, contributors and most importantly the listener will have felt that the coverage reflected the atmosphere and excitement of the day and that the outdoors had truly been brought inside.

According to Tony Bonner of Clipstore Ltd, who has engineered many OBs, setting up a typical day for a 7 pm broadcast means arriving on location at about midday.

> *First we would load the equipment into the room and rig, this would take about an hour or so. If the show is live via an ISDN you need to allow enough time for an engineer from the line company to come in site to fix any problems that may occur. 7 pm start the show, broadcast it live, end at 10 pm and allow an hour to de-rig and leave after checking you haven't left anything behind. If the programme is to be recorded only you just need to turn up a few hours before the public are allowed to enter the venue, rig and check everything is working as there are no worries about the ISDN. Once the show is over you will have to allow time to record any retakes of things like fumbled questions etc.*

The amount of equipment you would need to use depends on the type of programme. Let's look at one that involves a panel of experts answering questions put by members of an audience.

The OB van containing the mixing desk and recording facilities will be parked outside the hall. During the programme it will be occupied by the engineers who operate the equipment and the producer who will coordinate the performance. If the programme is to be broadcast live the team will communicate with the broadcast studio from the van and feed the programme via an ISDN line to the station studio. If it is a recording for later transmission it will be fed into a DAT machine or any other data-uncompressed stereo record format.

Inside the hall you need a microphone each for the host and the panel members and one or two mics to pick up the atmosphere, applause, laughter etc. from the audience. The roving mic used to pick up individual questions from members of the audience will often be radio mics to avoid long trailing cables. The mic would usually be carried about the hall to the questioner by a TO or BA. Another variation is to have a fixed mic on a stand and the questioners step up to it to speak. Any radio mic receivers and amplifiers would need to be in the hall as the OB van forms a shield that stops radio reception. You need a public address system (PA) so that the audience will be able to hear the proceedings, foldback via small speakers so the panel can hear what is happening and a talkback system so the producer can talk to the host via headphones and an on-air red light operated from the OB van outside to signal to everyone when you are live or recording. The signal from the hall and the power feed down a multicore to the van.

> *You have to be aware of Health and Safety during an OB. There are usually lots of long cable runs that need to be laid with the minimum risk of a member of the public tripping over them, being careful not to block fire exits etc. [says Tony Bonner]. A common problem can be having to find*

cables long enough to reach from a room to the OB van outside. We had an OB from Manchester Football Club and were on the sixth floor – our 50 metre cable was only just long enough. Extraneous noises such as air conditioning, public telephones, traffic can be a problem and it is easy to forget batteries for microphones and radios.

One of the skills that a radio broadcaster can develop and use in a number of different situations, particularly during OBs, is that of commentary. Basically you become the eyes of the listener and describe an event to them as it develops. Best known, of course, are sports commentaries and those during state occasions. If you think you may be good at it try muting the sound next time you are watching an event on television and provide the commentary yourself. It's not easy but it makes you realise how much research and information-gathering and note referencing is needed for a successful commentary.

Perhaps you should begin with a simpler task. You can do this with or without a portable recorder, but it is more educational if you can listen back to your efforts and analyse them later. Set yourself up at a vantage point to observe some human activity – a marketplace for example. Then describe aloud what you can see to an imaginary person sitting next to you who is blindfolded or someone who may be at the other end of a mobile phone. Begin by giving a general overview to establish where you are. Give more detail and help to create the picture in the mind of your listener by describing the scene from left to right or from the distant view to closer up. Then begin to zoom in on specific interesting activities and describe them in detail. Remember to mention colours, shapes and sizes in a form of words that will generate images. Don't feel you have to talk all the time as pauses will allow the listener to hear the natural sounds around them and give them time to mentally absorb the information you are giving them.

Commentary is a skill that can also be useful for reporters at the scene of an accident, demonstration or a public event, for example when they are asked to describe what they can see during a two-way.

Practice and soon you may be ready to grab your lip mic and head off to commentate on that World Cup match.

THE EXPERIMENTAL PROGRAMME

There are some radio stations that are outside the mainstream of broadcasting. There are some radio programmes that defy the usual heading or classification. There are some radio programmes that break the usual rules of production. There are some radio programmes that will be about subject matter that other programmes don't cover. To all these challenging areas we usually apply the term experimental.

To many this type of radio may be anarchic or at least different so its exposure on established stations is limited, but it flourishes on stations like Resonance FM which is London-based but is accessible via its web site. If you want to listen to radio that isn't formulaic and predictable then there are plenty of stations around whose schedules are devoted solely to experimental and creative radio that breaks the mould. Listen out too for the occasional experiment in genre or form on the mainstream networks like BBC Radio 4 and BBC Radio 3, but you may have to scan the listings magazines regularly to unearth the unusual among the regular output and be prepared to listen late at night where they are often placed in the schedules. Quite often the only way to tell if a programme is going to be different is if the station broadcasting it tells you by describing it, almost as a warning, as experimental. In the UK this kind of output is seen as a novelty rather than the norm and tends to be in the area of radio drama and comedy. Pioneering programmes cited as landmarks include the *Radio Ballads*, produced by Charles Parker, which combined voices, actuality and specially composed songs, *The Goon Show*, featuring surreal comedy, *Under Milkwood*, Dylan Thomas's play for voices, Samuel Beckett's play for radio *All That Fall*, Douglas Adams' *The Hitchhikers Guide to the Galaxy* (Sci-fi comedy) and Christopher Morris who combined comedy and music on Radio 1 in *Blue Jam*. The BBC Radio 3 series *Between the Ears* has brought listeners some of the most innovative programmes; in one the British painter Peter Blake took us on a journey in an old bus where he was joined by characters who peopled his imagination during his life including Elvis, Ian Dury and Kim Novak – where else but on radio could you experience such an entertainment? Stations like HIB 'Hearing is Believing', launched in Liverpool, which was touted as Britain's first experimental art radio station offered a wide range of off-the-wall programmes, its simplest being the sounds of birdsong with an accompanying spoken description of the bird taken from the *Observer Book of British Birds* and work by an exponent of radio art, Robin Rimbaud (better known as 'Scanner').

Let us not forget, however, that BBC local Radio was very much an experiment in local programming when it was launched in the 1960s as were many of the programmes tried for the first time on BBC network stations from the 1920s onwards. Much of what has been written on the subject of experimental radio or radio art refers to productions and stations in other parts of Europe, the USA and Canada.

If you are studying radio then the chances are that once the established methods of production and broadcasting are under your belt then you may be encouraged to experiment with the medium. Some educationalists believe that it is a good idea to encourage experimentation early in the learning process so that the results are reflected in more sophisticated work later in the course of study. Either way, if you get the chance to experiment then take it. Professional broadcasters often complain to me that they would love to have a go at trying something new but because of the pressure of workloads and deadlines to which they are already committed they lack the opportunity or encouragement from their supervisors. Broadcasting organisations want to employ people that can not only do the job that they were appointed to do but are creative and can contribute innovative ideas for programmes.

Here is a selection of exercises to get you thinking creatively and working experimentally:

- Choose a colour or a season. List the sounds, music and voices that you would use to depict your choice in an audio form. The voice material could, for example, include poetry or commentary.

- In the same way choose a selection of audio material that could be gathered to paint an audio portrait of a friend, relative or celebrity.

- Find a photograph and decide how you could represent the image in sound. For example a picture of a man throwing a stick for a dog on a beach is full of audio possibilities.

- If a radio reporter is sent to cover a new exhibition of work at an art gallery the content would usually contain things like an interview with the artist or gallery curator, a description of the work on display and perhaps the reactions of visitors. Can you think of a more imaginative way of covering the story? Again think about voices, music and sounds that may be available to you.

- Spend the day or night at a location in a city recording the actuality sounds generated by the people, transport and buildings. Mix and edit them together in a five minute 'soundscape' that reflects the atmosphere of the location. If you prefer to stay indoors record the sounds around your own home.

- Could you devise a format for a music programme that does not rely on presentation links from a DJ or back-to-back music tracks?

- Could you take an established and long-running programme that is still being broadcast on one of the network stations and devise a new format but keep the subject matter the same and keep the target audience listening week after week?

- If you have learned to make programmes using digital technology but you also have access to 'old technology' like tape recorders and tape editing equipment then get someone to show you how to use it and have a go at making a programme using the techniques employed by an earlier generation.

- Access an archive of radio programmes – many are commercially available on cassette and CD. Listen to a programme from the 1960s or 1970s and think about how you would remake it to appeal to a twenty-first-century audience. Would this involve a major rewrite of the script or a different style of production technique that may need to be applied? Ethically or legally would you want to change the content or the way the story is told? Are some of the jokes now regarded as non-PC and need to be rewritten?

6
A case study

A programme from idea to transmission

A programme starts as an idea which is then researched, developed, produced and finally broadcast. This case study follows a feature programme proposed by the independent production company Soundscape Productions (based in York) and commissioned by BBC Radio 4.

The First Song was broadcast to BBC Radio 4 listeners on 11 April 2002 at 11.30 am. Produced by Andy Cartwright and presented by singer Catherine Bott, this recorded production asked 'who or what sang the first song?' The programme process from idea to airing took about two years' work by the production team of producer, presenter, scriptwriter and technical support. The time span was unusually long because the proposal was resubmitted with variations after it was originally turned down.

Once the original idea had been approved by the company a proposal that would be submitted to the Commissioning Editor of the network is prepared. Then they wait for the next commissioning 'round' which starts when the commissioning editor provides a list of the sorts of programmes and programme series slots that the independent production companies will be invited to fill.

In 2004 BBC Radio 4 was commissioning 15,000 programmes across 14 different genres each year. The network runs a Registered Supplier List which is reviewed annually and will not consider ideas from independent companies not on the list.

All the BBC networks produce guidelines to suppliers which outline the slots available, the kind of programmes being looked for and guide prices. A deadline for proposals is set after which they draw up a shortlist. After discussions (the 'offers' meeting) on programme content, delivery dates and the budget the final list is drawn up.

It is imperative that the companies are fully aware of the network's audience and schedule. Their programme proposals need to reflect the network's aims to 'fuel the intellect and the imagination'. The companies also need to be sure that they can deliver on time and to stringent technical specifications. Like any other business they need to make sure that they will make a profit once they have paid all the staff involved, overheads and expenses so deciding and managing a budget is an important part of the process.

Preparing a proposal involves plenty of research time and documentation preparation. The Commissioning Brief issued to all Independent Production Companies states that:

- Proposals need to include a clear date for any topical peg that the programme may relate to. Proposals should also indicate which time-slot is thought appropriate for the programme.

- The proposal should be a brief synopsis that explains the focus of the idea with an indication of style and treatment.

- Suggested presenters should be included where appropriate with a note on whether they have been approached or involved in developing the idea. It is not essential to sign up a presenter before initial discussions with the Commissioning Editor.

- Proposals for series should give an idea of the breakdown into episodes.

The proposal is a selling document so needs to demonstrate why the network needs this programme, it should show evidence of research both of the topic and the potential audience, it should give an indication of how the programme will be structured, its content and its contributors, it should outline what questions the programme will ask and how it will answer them. The proposal will involve a lot of work if it is to successfully convince the Commissioning Editor that they should buy it for their listeners. Does the wording of the proposal enable the editor to hear that programme in their head? Will you be able to speak convincingly about your proposal and supply supplementary information off the top of your head if asked to do so at the offers meeting with the editor and his team?

Here is an extract from the 700 word proposal for *The First Song*:

> *The programme will be challenging but also entertaining. It will be a highly crafted piece of radio, which will weave together the presentational narrative with interviews, musical illustrations and actuality. Use will be made of aural comparisons by, for example, juxtaposing a child's song with whale song and cross-fading between the sounds of animal's and man's imitation of these sounds.*

The First Song started out as a proposal for a three-part series but as a result of feedback from the offers meeting it was resubmitted as a one-off feature. The programme was made up of links from Catherine Bott, clips from interviews with music ethnologists, scientists, scholars, musicians and singers plus of course music, sounds, animal calls and birdsong. Between the time of the proposal submission and the broadcast the choice of presenter and some of the originally named contributors had changed. This is quite common as sometimes they may not be available to take part or even approached at this stage. Names may be submitted to illustrate the calibre or qualifications of those who will eventually be contributing. The Commissioning Editor needs to be notified of any changes to the conditions laid down about contributors or material as part of the offer that the producers need to implement. However, in this case as in others the basic premise and quality of the programme remains the same with contributors of equal standing.

After the company have their offer accepted and are commissioned they need to start work on the production. Approaching and booking the presenter, getting copyright clearance for music performances and material, arranging and conducting interviews and editing their recorded material eventually working up that all important script. Here is a short extract from the thirteen page working script which was originally planned to run for 28′49″ but was eventually cut down to 27′41″. It contains links read by the presenter (CB), details of how a music extract and sound effect (FX) are to be included and clips from an interview with a composer (DF) plus the durations of these inserts and the time from the start of the programme they appear. So CB link 32 appears at 16 minutes and twenty-four-and-a-half seconds into the programme.

CB 32   16.24.30   The composer David Fanshawe (DF) burst onto the music scene in the early 1970s with his 'African Sanctus' – a dramatic blending of the English Choral tradition with his own recordings of indigenous music and traditional African songs.

Music   16.39   (Music fade up as before but add extra time so music up approx 16.30)

16.55.30   Since then Fanshawe has dedicated his life to recording ethnic music from all around the world (Pause)

17.06.30   And his studio in Wiltshire is an Aladdin's cave of tapes containing, he believes, some clues to the origin of song.

Music   17.08.30   (Music as before but add extra time so music up for approx 16.5 secs. Music up again to hit Sanctus hold at level until Deo then dip under so music up for approx 6.5 secs. Then be out by excelcis same place as before so music goes out earlier at 'by nature'.)

DF2b(i)	17.15	David Fanshawe

In: So much music that I have recorded . . .
Out: . . .with their voices.
Dur: 14″

FX	17.30	Chorus of Frogs

(Start under above as before but at this point we need to establish the frogs 2 or 3 croaks before dipping down.)

DF2b(ii)	17.34	David Fanshawe

In: I recorded frogs . . .
Out: . . .in central Africa.
Dur: 4″

Once the script is prepared, all the inserts edited and put into order, music, sounds etc. selected and timed it is time to go into the studio to mix the programme. Because this is going to be recorded any mistakes can be retaken and it can be edited or tidied up later. If a programme is to be mixed, all the sounds layered rather than simply being attached to each other, each sound needs to be available separately. In order to save time and demands on the presenter some segments that may be complex or are montaged together – that is to say mixed without a contribution from a presenter – can be mixed earlier and played into the final mix.

With the presenter in the studio at their microphone and the rest of the team in the control room they can begin recording and mixing the programme as outlined in the script. Depending on the content and complexity of the mix you can simply start at the beginning and rehearse a short segment then do it for real and record it. You carry on through the programme until the end.

The wording of the written trail submitted for use by the network summarises in a simple and concise way what is a complex programme and at the same time entices the potential listener.

Trail:

Tomorrow/This morning the singer Catherine Bott embarks on a remarkable journey in an attempt to discover who, or what, sang The First Song.
She travels back through time to the origins of music itself and into darkest pre-history. It's a journey that explores the significance of song, from medieval cathedrals to Stone Age monuments, and examines why the desire to sing is so fundamental to thousands of species – from the nightingale to the humpback whale.

So join Catherine Bott tomorrow/this morning at half past eleven as she talks to composers, biologists and archaeologists and tries to find out who sang – The First Song.

You will notice that the trail can be used the day before the programme is transmitted and earlier in the day of actual transmission.

The written presentation details or cue sheet submitted with the completed programme borrows on the wording and language used in the trail. This is the suggested opening announcement that would be read by the continuity announcer to introduce the programme:

Opening Announcement/Cue:

Even though we might not admit it – we all sing – even if it's only in the bath, or to ourselves in our heads. Singing is one of the most natural activities known to us humans.

But when did we start to sing and who, or what, discovered how we could do it?

In this morning's feature the celebrated singer Catherine Bott takes a journey back in time to try and find out who sang – The First Song.

The cue sheet then contains the details of the opening and closing words, music or sounds and the total duration of the recorded programme. This helps to inform the studio manager who is responsible for playing out the programme to check and confirm that they have the correct recording.

Here we can see that the programme starts with 19 seconds of music before Catherine introduces herself. At the end of the programme her closing words are '. . . still singing it' over music that ends rather than fades.

In: (Music 19") Hello, I'm Catherine Bott . . .
Out: . . . still singing it (music – ends)
Duration: 27'41"

There then follows on the cue sheet a suggested back announcement that the continuity announcer can read after the programme has finished.

Back Announcement/Out Cue:

The First Song *was presented by Catherine Bott and produced by Andy Cartwright as a Soundscape Productions for BBC Radio 4.*

In other words by using these announcements we are telling the listener what they are about to hear, then we let them hear it and then tell them what they have just been listening to.

Producer Andy Cartwright says that the secret of a good radio programme is the story and the storytelling. A listener may not have any interest in a particular topic or subject but if the story is told well they will become fascinated and involved. There are lots of different ways of telling a story on radio, a wide range of production methods, the producer is there to help the person telling the story to do it in the best way they can. Andy says,

> I knew I wanted a singer to tell the story. I think Catherine was a good choice, but I knew she would do a good job because she had experience of working in radio so she was able to contribute to the script, as a singer she had a personal interest in the subject and most importantly she was excited by the idea and content of the programme.

Andy's method of working with a presenter varies from programme to programme but generally he will discuss the script with them on a regular basis as it develops and will often let them hear the programme inserts in advance and try to make revisions well before the recording in the studio begins to save valuable studio time. On the day of recording he will usually avoid simply recording the presenter's links for cutting into the piece later, preferring to play in the inserts at the appropriate place during the recording. This method, similar to that used in a live programme, helps the presenter use their voice to give the script the correct tone and pace and conviction, enhancing the performance by giving it 'an air of discovery and freshness'.

Andy believes that a presenter is a presenter because they can present; they have a voice and personality for radio and it takes a certain type of ego to sit in front of a microphone and the producer needs to manage and massage that ego. The professional presenter should just be able to get on and do their job once the links have been rehearsed to everyone's satisfaction and guidance notes added to the script. They will know if they have stumbled, mispronounced or fluffed. Sometimes it is necessary for the producer to ask for retakes as they may not be aware of page turning noises, squeaking chairs, tummy rumblings or extraneous noises being picked up by the microphone.

It can take a little while to relax, get used to the microphone and get into the flow of the script so it can be a good idea to go back and record the opening links again at the end of the recording. Producers often record two versions of most links to give themselves a choice and some like to record the rehearsal too, again to offer more alternatives. Should you tell the presenter that you intend to record the rehearsal? It's up to you.

Unlike everyone else in the production team, who will generally stay focused on their particular contribution to the proceedings, the producer knows how the complete and completed programme should sound and needs to keep it in their mind the whole time. A producer never expects to be 100 per cent happy with the finished product. Availability of time, money, resources both human and technical will all conspire to thwart your efforts to achieve the effect you can hear in your head. There will be compromises. Some ideas will be dismissed for pragmatic reasons. You will be asking yourself how can I illustrate this point in a different way to save some money or time or who can I use to read this if so-and-so is not available?

All producers will in hindsight know how they would have done things differently. Andy, for example, would like to do a revised version of the opening of *The First Song*. At the time of the production he had in mind a particular effect but was unsure how to achieve it. Now, without the pressure of a deadline and production schedule he has finally worked out how it could be done.

> *However, not much changed between the original idea and the finished product. In essence the concept stayed the same it was the journey that was not expected. If you can summarise the programme in one sentence at the start of the production process then it should still be applicable at the end because that is the essence of the programme.*

Andy also believes that producers can get too close to their programmes.

> *Programmes become your babies; you really don't want to hand them over to someone else to produce when you have come up with an idea and are committed to it. But you should not be possessive or precious. Play the programme to someone whose judgement you trust and be prepared if you agree with their suggestions to change things. I did this with The First Song and ended up changing the mix to include more music and I think it is a better programme because of those changes.*

The First Song was produced by an independent production company and this puts extra demands on the small team. Although they provide some help and support you don't have the whole of the BBC behind you helping out with contracts and copyright issues or access to their research base.

This means things take longer and you need to factor this into your production schedule. Remember you are also likely to be working on a number of different projects at different stages of production or preparation at the same time.

If he is working on two programmes at the same time Andy tries not to allow the production timetables to overlap too closely, but during the production of *The First Song* a previous programme commission that had been delayed by a year in its production schedule because of the effects of the foot and mouth crisis in the Lake District was due to be broadcast a week earlier.

This time-shift meant that Andy had to oversee the mixing of both programmes during the same period. Time is finite and that puts production teams under pressure, but of course professionals make sure they meet their agreed deadlines and that the listener is oblivious to the problems encountered in the programme's production.

You will see on the script extract reproduced above some comments in brackets. These are Andy Cartwright's instructions to the editors, Clipstore Ltd in Leeds, who were responsible for editing and mixing the final programme. Warwick Pilmer insists that *The First Song* was a fairly straightforward edit job:

> Materials were supplied on DAT, CD and minidisk to be edited on SADiE classic (a mixing and editing software package). The programme is a fairly simple one; most of it contains a single recorded voice with a stereo wild track underneath which leads into music, actuality or another voice.
>
> The actuality is a mixture of real recordings, for example Dave Fanshaw had provided the sounds he recorded in Africa, and other sequences we created. After all there are no recordings of Stone Age man or of the big bang. We tried to make these sound as authentic as possible using a large selection of sound effects libraries. We had to make sure that the birdsong in the background was of a bird native to where that particular section of the programme is based. The big bang is a recording of a nuclear explosion. We also had to confirm a statement by a contributor that a whale song sounds like birdsong when speeded up before we could use the interview.
>
> Generally we mixed two to five audio tracks at once – a mixture of mono and stereo.
>
> I did a preliminary edit to get the materials off the DATs, CDs and MDs into SADiE and sequence them and de-um the speech parts (remove any unwanted umms and errs) which took about six hours.
>
> The whole editing and mixing process took thirty hours: however there are actually two versions (the original edit and the radio edit). This was because the producer decided to change the opening and closing sequences so that he could include more of the musical pieces.

The last word on *The First Song* goes to presenter Catherine Bott.

> I was pretty experienced at being a guest on a number of radio programmes on Radio 3 and Radio 4, but inexperienced when it came to presenting one, so I was flattered to be asked to do it. Andy sent me a copy of the script and I was allowed to make changes and customise it so that it 'sounded like me talking'. Script reading is different and difficult but now that I have learnt how to do it I am completely addicted and now want to try everything. What
> I hadn't realised was what it would lead to. Another producer heard the programme and thought I had a good turn of phrase and I was offered a short-term presentation contract with Radio 3. I found that I learn something

from everything I have done since and in turn everything I have done leads to being offered something else to do. I now feel confident that if The First Song was offered to me now I would enjoy being more involved in contributing to the writing of the script at an earlier stage. It was a real pleasure to work on the programme.

Glossary of radio programme-making terms

Some of these definitions are based on the glossary included in *Interviewing for Radio* (Beaman 2000). Due to the many changes in technology since it was published I have decided not to include terms that refer to the use of 'tape' in radio production including band, bulk eraser, cartridge, gash, ips, leader tape and open reel. Some words that continue to be used like splice, top and tail etc. that have been adapted or taken on new meanings are included in this new glossary. I acknowledge that alternative terms and meanings to the ones listed do occur even between stations and that new versions are entering the jargon even as you read this. It is important that you know the terms and shorthand that are used in broadcasting to ensure that you are able to communicate efficiently and accurately.

Acoustic   The way sound behaves in a particular environment. Indoors sounds are reflected or absorbed by the surroundings. A large empty room with high ceilings would produce a 'bright' acoustic. Rooms or spaces with bass-sounding acoustics are called 'boomy'. Studios are designed to produce a 'dead' acoustic.

Actuality   Sound recorded indoors or outdoors on location.

ALC/ARL   Automatic level control/automatic record level. A facility on some recording equipment which enables the input levels to be adjusted automatically rather than manually.

Angle   The particular approach a journalist will take to tell the story.

Atmos   Atmosphere. The natural or man-made background sounds or ambience present in a space that is used to establish the location of a broadcast or recording in the mind of the listener. For example the roar of traffic in a busy street, the echo inside a church or waves crashing on a beach.

Audio diary   Material recorded by a participant during the course of an event during which they comment and reflect on their activities.

Audio gatherers   People, both professional and trained amateurs, recruited to record the voices of the public for a major project or campaign by a station or network. For example the BBCs 2004 *Voices Project*.

Audio harvesting   The act of researching, storing and cataloguing audio from the archives for use in specific programmes or services.

Back anno   Back announcement. Information read by a programme presenter at the end of a broadcast item.

Backtiming   The process of timing a programme backwards from the intended end time to ensure it fits into its allocated slot.

Breakout box   A unit that allows equipment like an MD recorder to be linked to a computer so that recorded material can be downloaded for editing.

Bully   Bulletin. A news broadcast of a fixed duration and set time slot made up of copy, clips and voicers.

Cans   Headphones. Presenters wear cans in the studio so that they can listen to messages from another studio or source even when the microphone is open. Reporters will wear them when recording on location to check sound levels and quality. Contributors during discussions or phone-ins will need to wear them in order to hear the voices of callers on the phone or contributors based down the line in a satellite studio etc.

Clean feed   The signal sent to a caller taking part in a programme or recording on the telephone allowing them to hear the programme but not their own voice coming back down the line.

Clip   A short extract taken from an interview or actuality to be used as part of a news bulletin or programme taster. Also known as a 'cut'.

Clock   The running order and content of a programme hour represented in the form of a segmented circular clock face.

Commentary   An audio description of an event as it is happening by a reporter or correspondent. It can range from a football match or a royal wedding to a description of a simple activity.

Compliance   The process that questions and ensures that a programme is fit for broadcast.

Copy   Written text. A news story written to be read on air. Part of a script for a programme.

Copyright   The legal right of ownership of a written, recorded or designed piece of work.

Correspondent   A specialist reporter covering stories in a particular subject area, like education or a region of the country or overseas.

Cough key   A button on the studio table that can be operated by a presenter to cut the microphone temporarily should they need to cough.

Cue   (i) A hand-sign, verbal or indicator light signal to a presenter to start speaking.
(ii) A live introduction to a pre-recorded piece of audio. See also **Standard out cue** (SOC).

Cue sheet   The written introduction to a programme, feature, package or interview to be read by the presenter.

Cut   See **Clip**.

DAB   Digital audio broadcasting. The system used to transmit radio broadcasts digitally offering consistent and uniformly good reception. Operated from satellite and terrestrial transmitters it also allows for a larger number of stations to be carried than the analogue systems.

DAT   Digital audio tape. Cassettes that store recordings of sampled sounds that have been converted into a digital code.

Demo   Also known as demo tape or aircheck. A produced and packaged recording that contains a sample of the radio work of an individual or company demonstrating their abilities to a potential employer or client.

Demographic   The general profile or picture of the average listener to a radio station made up of a combination of particular characteristics like gender, age etc.

DJ   Disc jockey. A personality presenter of a music programme.

Documentary   A mainly speech-based programme that makes use of a range of audio material including interview, actuality, poetry, music, commentary, readings and sounds to tell its complex or multilayered story which is based on facts and contributions from credible witnesses.

Donut   (i) A musical jingle with a spoken ident or message at its centre.

(ii) A two-way with a recorded interview clip or vox pop played in halfway through.

Doorstepping   (i) The practice of journalists taking the opportunity to shout a question to a politician or celebrity as they pass in front of the assembled press pack.

(ii) The practice of journalists arriving unannounced at the home or workplace doorstep of a potential interviewee. Codes of Practice insist this technique should only be used if all other methods of obtaining an interview have failed.

Dub   To make a copy of a recording or transfer recorded material from one form of storage to another e.g. CD to MD.

Duration (Dur:)   The length of a broadcast or recording in minutes and seconds. It can refer to whole programmes, a music track, an interview clip etc. Two minutes and forty seconds would be written as 2′40″.

Edit   To shorten, remove or re-order audio material from a recording prior to broadcast. This is carried out using digital editing software on a computer. Audio tape can also be edited by cutting the tape with a blade and rejoining it with splicing tape. The term editing in context of the post of Editor also refers to the decision-making process to meet editorial policy standards.

ENPS   Electronic News Production System. The computer software used across the BBC news and programme production areas for news-gathering, archiving, story and script writing, running orders etc.

Fade   The effect of a sound being gradually reduced (fade down/fade out) or increased (fade up/fade in).

Fader   On audio mixing desks sliding the fader will increase or decrease the sound source allocated to it. Faders on BBC-designed and made mixing desks need to be pulled down towards you to open them and pushed up or away to close them. On commercial desks it is the opposite. Sometimes known also as 'pots' (potentiometers).

Feature   A longer form of recorded speech piece that focuses on one subject.

Feedback   Also known as 'howl-round'. A high-pitched noise generated when a sound emitting from a loudspeaker or headphones is picked up by the microphone that is the source of the original sound and feeds it through the speaker again. It can be avoided by making sure the loudspeaker is turned off or headphones kept at a lower level. It can also occur on air if a telephone contributor to a live programme has a radio switched on and tuned to the programme close to the telephone they are using to make the call. This can be avoided by asking the contributor to switch off the radio before you put the call to air. They will be able to continue to listen to the programme down the phone once they are put on hold.

Flip-flop   A style of double-headed presentation when links and stories are divided up and read alternately by the two presenters. It can also be used to describe the operational system when broadcast cubicles and studios are used alternately by consecutive programmes.

Freelance   A broadcaster or journalist who makes a living by working shifts or on short-term contracts for a range of different employers.

FX   Written instruction on a script to indicate the use of a sound effect. An effect created live in the studio is known as a spot effect (SFX).

GNS   General News Service. BBC newsroom which collects and distributes copy and audio clips to and from local radio newsrooms.

Gram library room, or in the case of BBC headquarters, department that catalogues and stores music recordings, sound effects and sometimes archive recordings at a radio station.

Grams   Refers to the playback machines in a studio used to play music, sound effects etc. on disc.

GTS   Greenwich Time Signal. The pips broadcast by the BBC to give an accurate time check, particularly on BBC Radio 4 leading up to the top of the hour.

Headlines   A short summary of the main news stories in a bulletin, usually one sentence for each story. Also referred to in some areas as a news summary.

Ident   Broadcast speech or jingle which identifies a radio station on air.

ILR   Independent Local Radio. Commercial local radio stations licensed and regulated by Ofcom.

INR   Independent National Radio. Commercial nationally available radio stations licensed and regulated by Ofcom.

Interview   Recorded or live question and answer session between journalist or presenter and a contributor. Research involves off-air interviewing of contributors.

Interviewee   Contributor who answers questions put by interviewer.

Interviewer   Journalist, presenter or researcher who poses the questions as part of an interview.

ISDN   Integrated Services Digital Network A system providing lines connected to a coder at one end and a decoder at the other that carry broadcast quality audio between studios or location to a station. For example each BBC local radio station will have an NCA (news and current affairs) studio which can be linked via lines booked with the traffic section in London. The lines are used to carry live audio without the interference experienced when using standard telephone lines.

Levels The measurement of the loudness of a voice or other sound source. Levels of all individual sound sources should be checked and adjusted if required prior to a recording or broadcast. Levels are measured by meters on the mixing desk; you should not rely simply on how it sounds through your headphones.

Link Spoken text that connects inserts, clips or music to others within a package, feature or programme.

Lip microphone Used mostly for commentary assignments, this microphone is designed to reduce the intrusion of loud background noise. The broadcaster positions it very close to the mouth with their top lip resting against a bar across the microphone.

Live Anything that is broadcast as it is performed directly to the listener. It can also describe a microphone that is switched on or any electrical equipment that is in operation.

Location Site away from the studio where an interview or programme may be recorded or broadcast.

Menu A list of items to be included in a programme. Read out by the presenter at the start of the programme.

Microphone rattle Unwanted noise picked up through the body or connector when operating a hand-held microphone. It can sometimes be eliminated by careful handling of the microphone, wrapping the cable loosely around your hand to avoid the disturbing the connections.

Mixing The combining and layering of separate pieces of audio using the controls of a mixing desk (or panel) or computer software. Links, for example, can be read over music or actuality. Successful mixes rely on appropriate levels being set for each individual sound source and the effective use of timings.

Montage A feature containing recorded audio material that is not linked by the voice of a presenter or reporter, but tells its story through the careful juxtaposition, superimposition and mixing of voices, music, actuality etc.

OB Outside broadcast. A live or recorded programme, part of programme or separate inserts from a location away from the studio.

Overnights Copy and other material left by journalists at the end of the day shifts for use by colleagues in the following early morning news bulletins and programmes.

Package A focused and creatively produced report for use in programmes. It will include reporter links with other audio like interview clips, music, actuality or vox pops. Also known as 'billboards' particularly on commercial radio who also use the term 'programme package' when referring to wraps.

P as B/P as R Programme as broadcast/programme as recorded. Documentation that must be submitted with BBC Network programmes to register music logs, script or running order, contributors' payments and confirms that a programme has been broadcast or recorded.

Phone-in   A programme that includes telephone contributions from listeners on the telephone.

Phono   A contribution to a programme from a reporter or interviewee on a telephone line.

Plugger   Someone who works for a record company who visits radio stations to promote their products. They provide promotional copies of CDs and information about their artistes for the station.

Podcast   A hybrid word combining elements of 'IPod' and 'broadcasting'. Audio produced by amateurs and some mainstream broadcasters made available for downloading onto listeners' MP3 recorders from their websites.

Popping   The breathy sound caused when a presenter or contributor is speaking too closely to a microphone. It is particularly noticeable when words beginning with plosive letters like p and b are used.

Pot cut/Pot point   To stop the playback of a recorded piece during broadcast at a convenient point, usually at the end of an answer or sentence, by sharply closing the fader on the mixing desk. The decision to pot cut, often because the programme may be heading for an over-run or other time constraints, is taken by the producer. However, efficient production teams will have asked reporters etc. to make a note on the cue sheet for the piece of any suggested pot point.

PPM   Peak programme meter. When told to 'watch your levels' this is what you should be looking at on the mixing desk to ensure that the output is not so high that it distorts or so low that it does not register. The meter is a calibrated dial on which the peak recording or playback levels of your programme or piece are indicated by a moving needle, thereby monitoring the broadcast or recording mix.

Pre-fade   The technique of starting a piece of music that will end a programme at a predetermined time so that it ends exactly on time. Often used when a programme uses a theme or signature tune. For example you have a three-minute piece of music which will close the programme so you start to play the track at exactly three minutes to the end of the programme but you do not open the fader to put it on air. The presenter finishes speaking at say thirty seconds to the close and the music is faded up for the final thirty seconds to neatly close the programme.

Pre-fade listen   Before committing an audio source to transmission or recording the sound levels are checked and adjusted before the fader is opened and the presenter, contributor, programme or item go on air. A switch (marked PFL – pre-fade listen) and a gain control knob to adjust the volume on the mixing desk enables the operator to play a short extract from the audio or speak into a microphone for a level check. They will see the levels register on the PPM and hear it on headphones.

Producer   The person in overall charge of a radio programme.

Profanity delay A facility used by commercial radio to avoid offensive callers being heard on air. It works by delaying the output of the station for a few seconds enabling enough time for the operator to cover over the comments with a station jingle.

Promo A station advertising campaign to promote itself on and off air.

PSA Public service announcement. Often produced in conjunction with a station's helpline or social action teams to draw public attention to a campaign like an aspect of road safety, blood donation etc. They will be broadcast free of charge by stations agreeing to feature them.

Radio car Vehicle equipped to transmit a broadcast signal from a location to a radio station enabling the operator to make a report into a programme, take part in a two-way or enabling the studio presenter to interview a contributor on site. It can also be used to transmit an outside broadcast programme. Radio cars are gradually being replaced with portable equipment that will do the same job using mobile phone technology.

RAJAR Radio Joint Audience Research. The company that collects, collates and publishes the listening figures of UK radio stations.

Recording The process of collecting and storing audio.

Risk assessment The process of considering any hazards that may cause problems for everyone involved in the production of a programme or item for a programme. The assessment should also bear in mind any ways the production could affect the general public.

ROT Recording off transmission. The recording of a live programme for re-broadcast or archiving. Also applies to the recording of a live interview during a programme that could be edited and used later in a news bulletin.

RSL Restricted Service Licence. A radio service granted a short-term licence to broadcast to a specific period and editorial area to provide news, information and entertainment as part of an event like an arts festival, conference or agricultural show.

Running order The order of items to be featured in a programme or news bulletin.

Satellite studio Outlying studio connected to a base local station. Usually well equipped for regular contributions to the main output but also capable of being used to opt out and broadcast to a specific editorial area. The studios are often staffed by a small team or district reporter. Stations covering large areas will have several satellite studios.

Script A radio programme in written form or the combination of several pieces of copy.

Segue Pronounced 'seg-way' this is the technique used in audio production when consecutive sounds or inserts are mixed directly from one to another without the use of a spoken link. It is a musical term that means 'follow on'.

Signposting Keeping the listener informed about items or guests that are 'still to come' or 'coming up later in the programme'.

Slug or catchline A word at the top of a piece of news copy or cue sheet which is used to identify the title allocated to the story. If it is a running or continuing story the same slug should be used on all documents.

Soundbite A short extract taken from a longer interview that differs from an ordinary clip in that it is particularly effective in summing up an opinion, experience, feeling or situation.

Splice Another word for an edit in an audio recording.

Standard Out Cue (SOC) An agreed closing statement used by a journalist at the end of a live or recorded report, e.g. 'Jim Beaman, BBC Radio News, Newcastle'.

Talkback An off-air intercom system that allows verbal communication between for example a producer in a studio and the presenter in the cubicle, newsreader in the news booth or a contributor in a satellite studio via their headphones or loudspeaker during a broadcast or recording.

Talkover When a presenter talks over the instrumental section of a piece of music before the vocals begin. The term is also applicable when a presenter or reporter speaks over a music bed or atmos.

Talk up A written trail for a programme or programme item coming up later in the day or programme read by the presenter.

Taster (or sometimes 'tease') An extract from a programme or item within a programme when used as part of the programme menu or trail.

TBU (also TCBU) Telephone balance unit (telephone control and balance unit) Studio equipment that allows linking a telephone line contribution to air when the call is transferred to the mixing desk for broadcast and balances the studio voice with that of the telephone voice.

Tone A single continuous sound played into the mixing desk and used to align and set the standard levels of the mixing desk. Known as zero tone it should register on a PPM at level 4.

Top and tail The start and end of a programme or item. It is usual to rehearse at least the top and tail of a live programme before going on air to check that everything and everyone is working OK. The term also refers to the editing or tidying up of the start and finish of a recorded item.

Traffic A BBC department that organises line and studio bookings for the NCA system. In commercial radio it is a department that organises the scheduling of advertisements for broadcast.

Trail (see also **Talk up**) Written or packaged information about a programme or programme item that can be heard later.

Two-way An interview between a presenter and a correspondent or reporter.

Voice piece Also known as a voice report or voicer. A scripted report written and read by a reporter or correspondent during a news bulletin or programme via the phone, on a recording, down the line or in the studio. A voicer can be a short report or a more considered longer analytical piece.

Vox pop   A selection of short comments voiced by the general public in response a question, recorded by a reporter in the street and edited together montage style.

Wildtrack   Background sounds and atmosphere recorded on location to add to the mix or act as a bed under a recording.

Windshield   A foam cover that is placed over the end of a microphone to help reduce distortion caused by air from a speaker's breath or wind noise on location.

Wrap   A scripted voice report that also includes one or two clips of illustrative audio, usually from interviews.

Zoo   The on air team who join the main presenter throughout the programme and make proactive and reactive contributions during the transmission.

References

Allen, John (2003) *BBC News Style Guide* London: BBC Training and Development.

BBC (2005) *Editorial Guidelines: The BBC's Values and Standards* London: BBC.

Beaman, J (2000) *Interviewing for Radio* London: Routledge.

Donovan, Paul (1997) *All Our Todays: 40 Years of the Today Programme* London: Jonathan Cape.

Greenwood, W and Welsh, T (2005) *McNae's Essential Law for Journalists* London: Butterworth.

Hendy, David (2000) *Radio in the Global Age* Cambridge: Polity.

Keith, M (2002) *Talking Radio. An Oral History of American Radio in the TV Age* New York: M. E. Sharpe.

MacGregor, S (2002) *A Woman of Today* London: Headline.

Ofcom (2005) *The Ofcom Broadcasting Code* London: The Office of Communications.

Ofcom (2005a) *Radio – Preparing for the Future* Phase 2 Implementing the Framework Section 3. Available at: www.ofcom.org.uk/consult/condocs/radio_reviewp2.

Purves, Libby (2002) *Radio: A True Love Story* London: Hodder & Stoughton.

Shapley, Olive (1996) *Broadcasting a Life – The Autobiography of Olive Shapley* London: Scarlet Press.

Shingler, M and Wieringa, C (1998) *On Air: Methods and Meanings of Radio* London: Arnold.

Starkey, Guy (2004) *Radio in Context* Basingstoke: Palgrave.

BBC Radio Newsroom web pages
www.bbc.co.uk/radionewsroom

BBC Commissioning Guidelines
www.bbc.co.uk/commissioning

BBC Recruitment
www.bbc.co.uk/jobs

BBC Editorial Guidelines
www.bbc.co.uk/guidelines/editorialguidelines

Office of Communications
www.ofcom.gov.uk

Radio Advertising and Sponsorship Codes and Guidance (compiled January 2005) including:
BCAP Radio Advertising Code
RACC Radio Copy Guidance
Ofcom Radio Sponsorship Rules

All quotes from Helen Galley, Andy Cartwright, Paul Jenner, Sarah Urban, Matt Horne, Alec Blackman, Jo Tyler, Katy McDonald, Gurindar Barar, Tony Fisher, Warwick Pilmer, Tony Bonner and Catherine Bott are from author interviews conducted face-to-face, via telephone or email in 2005/2006.

Quotes from Fran Acheson are from an author interview and bbc.training.com

Quote from Simon Nelson is from a presentation at the BBC's Innovation Day at Manchester, 12 January 2006.

'DJ in doomed bid to save life of caller who died on air' by Nigel Bunyan featured in *The Daily Telegraph*, Saturday 7 January 2006.

Between the Ears BBC Radio 3, 12 November 2005, 21.45 – 22.15.

SUGGESTED READING

Barnard, S (2000) *Studying Radio* London: Arnold.
Black, P (1972) *The Biggest Aspidistra in the World* London: BBC.
Briggs, A (1985) *The BBC: The First 50 Years* Oxford: Oxford University Press.
Cain, J (1992) *The BBC: 70 Years of Broadcasting* London: BBC.
Crisell, A (1994) *Understanding Radio* London: Routledge.
Crisell, A (2002) *An Introductory History of British Broadcasting* London: Routledge.
Crisell, A (ed.) (2004) *More Than a Music Box: Radio Cultures and Communities in a Multi-Media World* Oxford: Bergahahn Books.
Crook, T (1998) *International Radio Journalism* London: Routledge.
DeManio, J (1967) *To Auntie With Love* London: Hutchinson & Co.
Fleming, C (2002) *The Radio Handbook* London: Routledge.
Gilliam, L (1971) *Prospero and Ariel: The Rise and Fall of Radio* London: Victor Gollancz.
Glover, F (2002) *Travels With My Radio* London: Ebury Press.
Hicks, W (1998) *English for Journalists* London: Routledge.

McCrum, S and Hughes, L (1997) *Interviewing Children* London: Save the Children.

McWhinnie, D (1959) *The Art of Radio* London: Faber & Faber.

Mitchell, C (ed.) (2001) *Women in Radio* London: Routledge.

Norberg, E (1996) *Radio Programming Tactics and Strategy* London: Focal Press.

Poliakoff, S (1998) *Talk of The City* London: Methuen.

Scannel, P and Cardiff, D (1991) *A Social History of British Broadcasting, vol 1, 1922–1939* Oxford: Blackwell.

Street, S (2002) *A Concise History of British Radio* Tiverton: Kelly Publications.

Street, S (2004) *Radio Waves – Poems Celebrating the Wireless* London: Enitharmon Press.

Weiss, A (1995) *Phantasmic Radio* North Carolina: Duke University Press.

Weiss, A (ed.) (2001) *Experimental Sound and Radio* London: MIT Press.

The Radio Journal: International Studies in Broadcast and Audio Media Bristol: Intellect Books (published three times a year).

INFORMATION

These sites provide further detailed information about industry organisations, broadcasting regulations and guidelines that support and advise broadcasters.

Broadcasting, Entertainment, Cinematograph and Theatre Union (BECTU) www. bectu.org.uk

Broadcast Journalism Training Council (BJTC)
www.bjtc.org.uk

National Union of Journalists (NUJ)
www.nuj.org.uk

Skillset (The Sector Skills Council for the Audio Visual Industries)
www.skillset.org

Skillset and BECTU provide a careers service for those interested in broadcasting
www.skillsformedia.com

Radio Academy (Dedicated to the encouragement and recognition of excellence in UK radio)
www.radioacademy.org

Student Radio Association
www.studentradio.org.uk

The Radio Magazine
www.theradiomagazine.co.uk

Hospital Broadcasting Association
www.hbauk.com

National Sound Archive (British Library)
www.nsa.co.uk

IRN Independent Radio News
www.irn.co.uk

Department of Media, Culture and Sport
www.culture.gov.uk

Law and student media
www.nusonline.co.uk/studentmedia

Community Media Association
www.commediaorg.uk

Commercial Radio Companies Association (CRCA)
www.crca.org.uk

Radio Advertising Bureau (RAB)
www.rab.co.uk

The RAB and CRCA will join forces under a new umbrella organisation in 2006. The new body will bring all commercial radio company interests under one roof for the first time and will include a commissioning centre charged with making programmes for broadcast across the entire commercial radio network. It will be called The Radio Centre and can be contacted at CRCA at 77 Shaftsbury Avenue, London W1D 5DU.

Advertising Standards Authority
www.asa.org.uk

Broadcast Committee of Advertising Practice
www.cap.org.uk

Radio Advertising Clearance Centre
www.racc.co.uk

You can get information about radio programmes that are recorded in front of audiences, and usually free tickets, by contacting the station staging the recording. In the case of BBC shows contact radio.ticket.unit@bbc.co.uk.

Your comments and views about programmes you have heard on BBC radio services may be featured on BBC Radio 4's programme *Feedback*. Email: feedback@bbc. co.uk; Tel: 08700 100 400 (7 am–midnight).

Index

Related titles in the Media Skills series

Designing for Newspapers and Magazines

Chris Frost

Designing for Newspapers and Magazines examines how newspapers and magazines are produced. It offers guidance on how to produce attractive publications and how to tailor them to their target audience by advising on the use of colour, text placement, typography and images.

Designing for Newspapers and Magazines shows how a well-designed publication can provide a powerful platform for good journalism. Written by an experienced journalist and designer, the book details the elements of good design and provides instruction on how to get the most out of computers and computer-aided design. A final section examines a range of different local and national publications and explains the reasoning that underpins their design choices. *Designing for Newspapers and Magazines* includes:

- How to set up a new publication
- Planning an edition of a newspaper or magazine
- Typography and working with text
- Working with images and technical production
- Design pages and how to use colour
- Design and journalism ethics
- A glossary of journalistic and design terms

ISBN 10: 0–415–29026–0 (hbk)
ISBN 10: 0–415–29027–9 (pbk)

ISBN 13: 9–78–0–415–29026–5 (hbk)
ISBN 13: 9–78–0–415–29027–2 (pbk)

Available at all good bookshops
For ordering and further information please visit:
www.routledge.com

Related titles in the Media Skills series

Ethics for Journalists

Richard Keeble

'Richard Keeble's book asks questions which dominate our working lives and it is invaluable not just to working journalists and students, but to the reading and listening public on whom our work depends.

There isn't a journalist who would not benefit from reading this book especially if he or she attempts to answer some of the questions in it.' – *Paul Foot*

Ethics for Journalists tackles many of the issues which journalists face in their everyday lives - from the media's supposed obsession with sex, sleaze and sensationalism, to issues of regulation and censorship. Its accessible style and question and answer approach highlights the relevance of ethical issues for everyone involved in journalism, both trainees and professionals, whether working in print, broadcast or new media.

Ethics for Journalists provides a comprehensive overview of ethical dilemmas and features interviews with a number of journalists, including the celebrated correspondent Phillip Knightely. Presenting a range of imaginative strategies for improving media standards and supported by a thorough bibliography and a wide ranging list of websites, *Ethics for Journalists* considers many problematic subjects including:

* The representation of women, blacks, gays and lesbians, and the mentally ill
* Controversial calls for a privacy law to restrain the power of the press
* Journalistic techniques such as sourcing the news, doorstepping, deathknocks and the use of subterfuge
* The impact of competition, ownership and advertising on media standards
* The handling of confidential sources and the dilemmas of war reporting

ISBN 10: 0–415–24296–7 (hbk)
ISBN 10: 0–415–24297–5 (pbk)

ISBN 13: 9–78–0–415–24296–7 (hbk)
ISBN 13: 9–78–0–415–24297–4 (pbk)

Available at all good bookshops
For ordering and further information please visit:
www.routledge.com

Related titles in the Media Skills series

Freelancing for Television and Radio

Leslie Mitchell

.

Freelancing for Television and Radio explains what it means to be a freelance in the world of the audio visual industries. From an outline of tax and employment issues it goes on to describe the ups and downs of the world in which the freelance works. Radio, television and related sectors like facilities and video production are assessed for the opportunities they offer the aspiring freelance, and there's also an analysis of the skills you need for a successful freelance career.

Freelancing for Television and Radio includes:

* Practical advice on how to make a start; where to find work; writing the right kind of CV, networking and making contacts
* Important section on maintaining and developing a freelance career as well as a chapter on the challenges and responsibilities of setting up and running a small business.
* A significant chapter on the basics of writing and submitting programme proposals to broadcasters as well as a substantial section of useful contact information.

ISBN 10: 0–415–34101–9 hbk
ISBN 10: 0–415–34102–7 pbk

ISBN 13: 9–78–0–415–34101–1 hbk
ISBN 13: 9–78–0–415–34102–8 pbk

Available at all good bookshops
For ordering and further information please visit:
www.routledge.com

Related titles in the Media Skills series

Interviewing for Radio

Jim Beaman

'This is an invaluable guide to radio interviewing of all kinds, from the vox pop to the full-scale discussion. I learned a lot.' – Sue Lawley, *Desert Island Discs, Radio 4*

'Impressively up to date, and full of excellent tips for both novices and the old hands too.' – Sue MacGregor, *Today, Radio 4*

Interviewing for Radio is a thorough introduction to the techniques and skills of the radio interview. It offers advice on how to ask the right question and elicit a response and guides the reader through the use of equipment, the mechanics of recording, the studio environment, live broadcasts, presentation and pronunciation and editing material.

Interviewing for Radio critically analyses previously broadcast interviews and together with advice from radio professionals explains the preparation, organisation and communication required to produce a successful radio broadcast. Written by an experienced producer, presenter and instructor, *Interviewing for Radio* includes:

*   the history of the radio interview and the importance of its role today
*   practical exercises which introduce successful interview and technical skills
*   case studies and hypothetical scenarios to help prepare for potential difficulties
*   a discussion of ethics, risk assessment, codes of conduct and safety issues
*   a glossary of radio and broadcast terms, further reading and suggested listening.

ISBN 10: 0–415–22909–X (hbk)
ISBN 10: 0–415–22910–3 (pbk)

ISBN 13: 9–78–0–415–22909–8 (hbk)
ISBN 13: 9–78–0–415–22910–4 (pbk)

Available at all good bookshops
For ordering and further information please visit:
www.routledge.com